NEL... ...
THE GOLDEN ORB

A Life
&
Sonnet Sequence

by
John Twells

NELSON: THE GOLDEN ORB

A Life & Sonnet Sequence

Published in 1995 by Ownart Ltd,
15 Church Lane,
Darley Abbey,
Derby DE22 1EX.
Telephone 01332 557121 Fax 01332 559358

© John Twells 1995

The right of John Twells to be identified as Author of the Work has been asserted by him in accordance with the Copyright, Designer and Patents Act 1988.

All rights reserved. No part of this publication may be reproduced in any form or by any means – graphic, electronic or mechanical, including photocopying, recording, taping or information storage and retrieval systems without the prior permission in writing of the author except for brief quotations for a book review.

ISBN 0 9523440 0 9

Covers illustrations copyright
© The National Maritime Museum,
Greenwich, London SE10 9NF,
England
Telephone 081 8584422 Fax 081 3126632

Printed in 10/11½ point Cheltenham typeface and produced by
Stott Brothers Ltd, Colour Printers,
Lister Lane, Halifax,
West Yorkshire HX1 5AJ,
England
Telephone 01422 362184 Fax 01422 353707

THE GOLDEN ORB

PART I	1–34	WIDE HORIZONS *Childhood: Arctic: Ganges: America: Caribbean*	1758–87
PART II	35–66	SPANISH TRIUMPH & DISASTER *Cape St. Vincent: Tenerife*	1788–97
PART III	67–90	THE BAND OF BROTHERS *The Nile*	1798
PART IV	91–116	A FOREIGN COURT *Naples*	1798–1800
PART V	117–150	THE NORTHERN THREAT *Copenhagen: The Baltic*	1800–01
PART VI	151–188	THE LONG CHASE *The Mediterranean: West Indies*	1801–05
PART VII	189–218	TRAFALGAR	1805

WIDE HORIZONS

1758–87

WIDE HORIZONS

1   In the beginning under high wide skies   *1758–67*
            Above long seas beside the Norfolk coast
            At home he heard his father emphasise
            Faith. Duty. Father, Son and Holy Ghost.

            How duty done ensured reward to come
            Not presently but at some future time
            Assured as honey followed from the hum
            Of summer bees about a flowering lime.

            Or as a gusting wind in winter, cold
            With snow showers from the north and east,
            Swirled draughts around the rectory's linenfold
            Yet raised up visions of the Christmas feast.

            So warmed by hope of happiness and fed
            On faith in things to come the boy was bred.

2   A kindly household filled with cheerful noise
            A clamour quietened as the father's voice
            Recited grace or ordered girls and boys
            To sit straight spined at table and rejoice.

            The roots drilled deep from which these children grew
            Viking and Anglian with a Saxon strain.
            Their mother's cousin, Premier Walpole, threw
            A light upon the height they might attain.

            No pitying of self could whelm a boy
            With seven siblings as the Christmastide
            When he was nine brought grief instead of joy
            And on the Boxing Day their mother died.

            Eleven times in childbirth she gave breath.
            A daughter said she had been bred to death.

The Rev Edmund Nelson

WIDE HORIZONS

3 Her rector husband Edmund often claimed   1767
   He lacked the worldliness the world required
   To "bring the children forward" yet he blamed
   Himself unduly for the brood he sired

   For underneath his roof good order taught
   Both self and mutual help. There common sense
   Prevailed, with firm but kindly Christian thought
   And scholarship more plentiful than pence.

   Thence in its early teens each child was sent
   To learn a trade and so to earn its keep.
   A naval clerk, a milliner, each went
   Well sheathed by faith to swim upon the deep.

   Hammered with love and shaped as by a smith
   By this tall monger of religious myth.

4 The sixth child and the third surviving son   1770
   Horace to friends, Horatio to his sire
   At twelve sought service with the sword and gun
   Bedecked between the deep sea and the fire.

   One sword, a talismanic legend, came
   To Captain Suckling by distaff descent
   Inspired a nephew's boyish dreams of fame
   And pointed to the path on which he went.

   That sword was carried when a Walpole lost
   An arm against the French in Vado Bay
   And still, in storm and darkness, was to cost
   Another limb upon another day.

   The sword, rough seas, oak ships and threatening France,
   His mother's bete-noire, offered him his chance.

WIDE HORIZONS

5   These and the need for placement stirred the child   *1770*
To ask bluff uncle Suckling for a post
Despite the looming warfare and the wild
Hazards of wreck upon a leeward coast.

"What has poor Horace done that is so weak
That he above the rest should now be sent
To rough it out at sea?" His letters speak
Of Suckling's doubts and, later, his content.

"But let him come and the first time we go
To action then perhaps a cannon ball
Will knock his head off and in doing so
Provide for him at once!" No clarion call

But robust humour of the rougher sort
Conned this small Norfolk schoolboy out of port.

6   In "Raisonnable" an elfin midshipman   *1771–3*
Watched her refit against a threat from Spain
Thus on a captured French ship's deck began
A life of conquest, servitude and pain.

On sea skills all his later dramas turned
A mastery of canvas, rope and wood
Of men, of tide, wind, time and currents learned
In deep or shoal betwixt the ebb and flood.

Shrewd Suckling furthered this apprenticeship
By sending him aboard a merchantman
Upon a long West Indian trading trip
That crossed the Carib Sea to Yucatan.

The master, once in "Dreadnought", taught how charts
With sun, clock, stars and sextant played their parts.

WIDE HORIZONS

7   Home to his uncle's "Triumph", 74,   *1773*
       The guardship for the Thames and Chatham based
       Where all his confidence to sail inshore
       Was nurtured, so he wrote, from trials he faced.

       The sandbank navigation at the Nile
       From Thames and Medway cutter work arose
       A boatcrew's care, for boys, as big a trial
       As tacking fleets to Admirals can pose.

       At 14, once again a volunteer,
       He set himself to dance a different jig
       From Deptford sailed, a coxswain, charged to steer
       In Arctic seas a bomb sloop captain's gig.

       The midnight sun sank lower and a vice
       Gripped "Carcass" and her sister ship in ice.

8   No North West Passage opened but at dawn   *1773*
       In mist and fog seen dimly on the floe
       The outlines of a bear and boy were drawn
       Upright beside a crevice in the snow.

       His musket snapped but failed to fire its ball
       Yet as the boy continued still to stand
       A cannon fired to warn, deter, recall
       And brought him back to face a reprimand.

       "I wished to kill the polar bear and take
       Its skin back to my father." Nelson said.
       Swift orders followed. "Drag the boats and make
       For open sea. Each take two stones of bread."

       A sudden turbulence unclamped their vice,
       Strong winds arose and broke the locking ice.

WIDE HORIZONS

9 A crowded month at home. Thence "Seahorse" bore *1773–6*
   Him round the Cape to Basra and Ceylon
   A voyage he started in good health, though poor
   But finished fevered and with cash he won.

   £300 in one night's gaming came.
   His dawn reaction was "What if I'd lost?"
   The resolution never more to game
   Not hard for one who had to count the cost.

   The price of service, though, he reckoned not.
   Malaria felled him and he nearly died
   Delirious in a swinging canvas cot
   All thought would shroud him sliding overside.

   From Sunderbuns to Solent slowly sailed
   The "Dolphin" as his fearful fever failed.

10 The throb, the sweat, the reeling of the brain *1776*
   The rantings, shivers, visions, fears and pain
   The frissons, tremors, sickness and the stain
   On skin of salty sweat lines came again

   Again, again, again, the tertians came
   Each side of deep depressions and the rain
   Of pouring sweat from an ill-nourished frame
   For ever waxed and never seemed to wane

   Until, near death, the fluid's source was dry
   The simmering brain, the racing pulse ran slow
   And psychodelic circlings on the eye
   Were coalesced into an inner glow.

   "My orb." he called it, round and shining gold,
   Beckoning to fame and bidding him be bold.

WIDE HORIZONS

11   The inward light which now suffused his mind   *1776*
Unlike conversion near the Street called Straight
Which Saul experienced was in truth a kind
Of confirmation of both faith and fate.

An affirmation to the King he served
Surrendering thought of self in hope of fame
A fame bestowed on those who fame deserved
By selfless service through the fire and flame.

A lifelong vision. Hardy later heard
"My orb" referred to as a fierce belief
In King and Country which inspired and spurred
To excellence and smothered worldly grief.

The body purged, a spirit scourged and lashed
From negative to positive had flashed.

12   The "Worcester" rolled, she slid, she climbed, she shook   *1776–7*
The spume from yards on cresting each long sea
Her tackle squeaked, her timbers creaked, she took
The strain of sleet squalls whipping out to lee.

The slatting rigging and the soughing shroud
The smack and bulge of half brailed sodden sail
The pitching convoy glimpsed through scudding cloud
Then screened behind a stinging belt of hail.

The sea, wind stirred to anger, foamed and heaved
Above her bow and sluiced her weather side
And soused the cross-deck lifelines stoutly reeved
Where those who missed their grip or footing died.

No heat of fever now but seasick chill
To threaten, forge and test a seaman's will.

WIDE HORIZONS

13   A trans-Atlantic escort, not 'first rate',   1776–7
"Worcester" was apt and strong enough to scotch
Frigate or privateer and educate
An Acting 4th Lieutenant standing watch.

Set for Gibraltar, south across the Bay,
French squadron haunted or, when standing west,
At risk of grounding on some unknown cay.
Mankind and nature obviated rest.

The constant discipline, the trials endured
Preserved Canadian and West Indian trade
While British links with India were ensured
And long neglected naval power re-made.

But truths ignored and dithering debates
Split Britain from the later greater States.

14   Six years sea service. Next, the Navy Board.   1777
Enquiring Captains faced and satisfied.
Appointment followed. Then he could afford
The portrait which displays him steady eyed

Upright. Broad level brows. A strong, long nose
Wide sensual lips by discipline compressed
Full lower lip, broad jaw, firm chin compose
A face with lurking laughter half suppressed.

Yet laughter lives there as do love and art
Creative traits, capacities half seen
Requiring subjects for that ardent heart
To work upon. He was but yet eighteen

Proud in cocked hat, a blue coat edged with gilt
And both hands clasped upon the long sword's hilt.

WIDE HORIZONS

15   "Our sugar islands" George IIIrd declared   *1778*
"Must be defended even at the risk
Of France invading England." Those who shared
West Indian dangers also shared the brisk

Business in prizes taken on the Main.
Lieutenant Nelson from the "Lowestoft"
Boarding one wallowing sloop was washed again
Across her bulwarks but then sent aloft

The British colours. Quick promotion came.
He cruised in "Little Lucy" in command,
A captured schooner, one small step to fame,
Towards "Victory", loss of life and eye and hand

Via dead men's shoes in "Bristol" and his big
Jump to Commander in the "Badger", brig.

16   That dreadful ethos of the men of war
Which takes from servitude a murderous pride
Possessed the British navy to its core
And mattered more the more their shipmates died.

War with America, with France, with Spain
In small ship actions honed their killing skill
Each death, each wound, each sickness, every pain
Stern reinforcement for each seaman's will.

The ship, the service and the flag unstained
Each crew sustained and strove with storm and foe
To live; to win. By competition trained
To ride out blasts or strike the heavier blow.

Fierce discipline implanted from above
Fired every crew. But Nelson added love.

WIDE HORIZONS

17   A love which from enthusiasm rose   *1778*
And offered each a spiritual beauty
The feeling that fulfilment came to those
Who gloried in submission to their duty.

A servitude which triumphed over fear
Subdued both flesh and self and brought success
To British seamen once they learned to steer
Across the reef of each man's selfishness.

With that accomplished all potential power
Was harnessed to a naval captain's will;
His seamanship, his judgement and the flower
Of all his crew, his gunners' speed to kill.

At twenty eager Nelson led small crews –
Then stepped into a dead Post Captain's shoes.

18   Desire for honours and pursuit of wealth
Meant death made openings for others
While greater risks to life and limb and health
More strongly forged that chain of naval brothers.

A shot which killed brought Nelson rank and pay
"I most sincerely hope" he later wrote
"That when I go I leave the world that way."
Old age ashore less sought than death afloat.

But his first Captain's service was on land
At Kingston when Jamaica faced attack
The battery at Fort Charles a mixed command
Of soldiers and civilians white and black.

D'Estaing's armada north from Haiti sailed
Ignored Jamaica and off Georgia failed.

WIDE HORIZONS

19   His frigate "Hinchingbrooke", a 28,   *1779–80*
Was ordered escort to a minor force
Despatched ill found and far too late
To miss foul weather or affect the course

Of war with Spain. Malaria and the hosts
Of stinging insects, mud and yellow jack
And tree trunks rotting in Mosquito Coast's
Snake ridden rivers held their movement back.

Up stream the redcoats straggled to attack
St Juan, the Nicaraguan choke-point fort
And captured it but sickness and the lack
Of fresh supplies brought everything to nought.

200 crew with Nelson marched. He spurned
His fevers laying guns. Ten men returned.

20   Relapsing fevers were a constant curse   *1780*
Throughout his service and when borne ashore
And carried to a freed Jamaican nurse
She could not cure but managed to restore

His partial health to let his work expand
In two-faced "Janus", new, a 44,
That looked both fore and aft a fine command.
At twenty one he could not hope for more.

Morbidity, malaria unsuppressed;
Seasickness, colic, cramp, stomachic pain
Drained all his energy and strength. Distressed
He begged for English leave to end the strain.

And from Port Royal the frigate "Lion" bore
Towards England England's hardiest cub of war.

WIDE HORIZONS

21   In Woolwich Dockyard "Albermarle", once called   1781–2
"La Menagere", was strengthened and transformed
From merchantman to frigate, guns installed,
Flag hoisted and commissioning performed.

From Copenhagen sailed her merchant fleet
Which fetched the Navy's Baltic spar and mast
But pitched off wintery Yarmouth incomplete.
A raiding privateer had proved too fast.

Slow "Albermarle" then bucked about the Downs
In contrary winds. The drifting "Brilliant" rammed
The anchored former Frenchman and the Crown's
New frigate Captain, calm but angry, damned

Her flimsy build which added to his cares
Three wasted months in Portsmouth for repairs.

22   From Cork a grey Atlantic's heave and swing   1782
Of long ridged undulations flicked and flecked
By wind or stormy petrel's planing wing
Raised fear of half a vanished convoy wrecked.

Three thousand miles ranged "Albermarle" at large,
From "Daedalus" parted in the dark and wrack,
As scattering gales dispersed their errant charge
While struggling to whip in the straggling pack.

Yet staggering slowly through an evil sea
In dribs and drabs all found that iron strand
And narrow harbour lined with cliffs to lee,
St John's, the gate to Britain's Newfoundland

Where Cabot's ships were "stayed" by shoals of cod
And Gilbert in a gale was near to God.

WIDE HORIZONS

23   In face of dangers all men will combine,   *1782*
And seas impose a discipline through fear,
Yet lift constraints and foolish men align
Against the neighbours whom they once held dear.

Or when presuming on an ancient right
Ignoring change and growth and common sense
Resort to arms and in a civil fight
Kill kin and squander dollars, pounds and pence.

Thus then America and Britain fought
Their fratricidal and spasmodic war
In which presumptuous arrogance was taught
Humility at Yorktown but before

The peace was signed young Nelson found at sea
How fruitful kindly courtesy can be.

24   In Boston Bay Nathaniel Carver ran
His "Harmony" for home near Plymouth Rock
But Nelson stopped the Massachusetts man
And took his schooner prize with all its stock.

Then pressed him as a pilot for the Bay
Bespattered with its shallows, shoals and banks.
That service rendered, sent him on his way,
Returned the vessel, certified his thanks.

Next, with new knowledge, played at hide and seek
With five large warships newly come from France
And found safe refuge in a narrow creek
To end "a pretty nine or ten hours dance".

Unbidden, Carver brought fresh greens and meat
When they had nothing but 'salt horse' to eat.

WIDE HORIZONS

25 A weariness, depression, muscle ache,   *1782*
    Soft gums, eyes sunken in a sallow face,
    Hallmarked his scurvied crew and made him make
    A hurried passage to Quebec, a place

    Of blazing beauty in the sharp aired fall
    Of gold and scarlet leaf, bright, whitening sky,
    A citadel, a gated city wall
    Steep streets and deep St Lawrence sliding by.

    A month's fresh food made all his seamen fit
    As Nelson in the social round took part
    Rime limned his rigging, masts by frosts were lit,
    But stately Mary Simpson thawed his heart.

    To plight her, then sixteen, he came ashore.
    Friends intervened and turned him back to war.

26 The ice closed down the river at his stern
    The ice crimped canvas, rope and skin to wood
    But all his convoyed transports lived to earn
    Him praise and commendation from Lord Hood

    Who lay by Staten Island off New York
    Where, prophet and reporter, Nelson wrote
    That money was the subject of all talk
    The one "great object" of all men of note.

    He seemed, with long, fair and unpowdered hair
    "A boyish captain" to a future king
    A midshipman who with his bulbous stare
    Sensed genius and the future it might bring

    To Britain and the whole world if by chance
    Discord should turn to tyranny in France.

WIDE HORIZONS

27 Prince William noted Nelson overdressed   1783
    When asking Hood's permission to transfer
    To his command but found the Admiral stressed
    That he for naval knowledge should refer

    To this young captain. 'Tactics for a Fleet'
    Were his especial skill, his knowledge bought
    By study but in practice incomplete
    As he had never in such action fought.

    The Peace of Paris signed, Prince William steered
    Home via Havana, Nelson as his guide.
    All "Albermarle's" ship's company volunteered
    To sail with him again. He quietly cried

    And for his men's back pay in London fought.
    His Admiral presented him at Court.

28 Peace brought him leave. With unfulfilled intent   1783–4
    He spent the winter in the North of France
    To learn the language, an accomplishment
    Of use at sea or in the social dance.

    Impatience foiled him. But he saw the lack
    Of middling folk; thought one post inn a "sty",
    Its horses merely "rats" and sensed the black
    Abyss between the rich and poor; the cry

    Of "Liberty" choked back in starving throats.
    Miss Andrews claimed his vulnerable heart;
    Cash cautious, he declined to burn his boats
    And, dowerless, the couple chose to part.

    His new ship "Boreas", apt name, set sail
    "Bride seizer, monarch of the northern gale."

WIDE HORIZONS

29   On peaceful passage westward "Boreas" bore   *1784*
Both wives and daughters toward the Leeward Isles
With 30 midshipmen to train for war
Upon calm seas amid seductive smiles.

Young Captain Nelson supervised their school
And led their sun and sextant work at noon
And to each nervous boy applied his rule
Of leadership declaring that they soon

Would meet at masthead in a rigging race.
Once there via lubbers' hole or futtock shroud
Each child beside his captain's smiling face
Looked down on deck and fear and laughed aloud,

Humanity, strict service, humour, such
Ingredients spiced the ripening Nelson touch.

30   The cone of Nevis rises from the Main
A thousand metres, circular and green
Where coconut and lime and sugar cane
Flower in a tropic landscape layered between

The blue of sky and that sapphiric blue
Of narrow strait above a channel dark
Beside St Kitts where shadows passing through
Are sauntering tarpon squadrons or a shark.

And there the booby scoops with bill absurd
While rainbow glistenings from the flying fish,
Droplets afire, may match the humming bird,
A jewelled flash upon its nectar dish.

On duty there this ardent captain came
And beauty sought to match incipient fame.

WIDE HORIZONS

31   'Les enfants poussent toujours' the French declare   *1785*
And lusty Nelson landed with intent
To seek a bride but also with a care
For rectitude and the establishment

Prevailing in the British Antilles.
Thus, waiting on the Council's President
He met a boy of five and on their knees
They played beneath a table, an event

From which young widowed Mrs Nisbet gained
A first impression which was excellent
And wrote to thank him. Nelson thus obtained
An entree and because on marriage bent

Embraced the son as if he were his own,
A link enduring when the child was grown.

32   Plantation life, as in the southern States,
For whites in Nevis flourished but was based
On luxury which slavery creates
Enjoyed by those whose ancestry was traced

To Britain's fringes. Nisbet claimed descent
From Scottish kings. His Woolward widow grew
From trading seamen who for betterment
Sailed westward with a sturdy Suffolk crew

And on the island which Columbus found
Judge Woolward married with a younger line
Of Pembroke's earls, the Herberts, there renowned
As senior partners in a trade combine.

Their girl, whom Nelson wed but later banned,
Was christened at St George's, Gingerland.

WIDE HORIZONS

33   Frances, or Fanny, grew; a handsome child   1785–7
Well schooled in French and English and well read.
A painter, needlewoman, mother, mild
But tough, with parents and a husband dead.

The courtship, formal, earnest and prolonged
Was interrupted when the "Boreas" cruised
Among the islands. Nelson, silver tongued
And fervid in his letters felt abused

When Yankee skippers sued him. He restrained
Their trading with the islands which before
The war was legal. Islanders complained
But he enforced the Navigation Law.

Prince William, Captain now, insisted on
Being bride's 'father' at Fig Tree St John.

34   When ordered home the "Boreas" returned   1787–9
With Nelson sickly to an England cold
But peaceful where the couple quickly learned
The discipline of half-pay. National gold

Most frugally dispensed in time of peace
Kept ships paid off and officers ashore.
They visited old friends and sought a lease
Sojourned in Bath and loved the Exmouth Moor.

The Burnhams and the county whence he came
Reclaimed their own. He dammed the Rectory stream
And with Josiah his step-son played a game
With model warships to reflect a dream

Of high command and children of his own
Which for frustrated talent would atone.

SPANISH TRIUMPH
&
DISASTER

1788–97

SPANISH TRIUMPH & DISASTER

35   He spent five years of boredom 'on the beach'   *1787–92*
Punctilious in his care for home and wife
And weekly heard his ageing father preach
Rectorial rectitudes on country life.

She for her part cared deeply for both men
But Norfolk's bitter winter winds reviled.
Ensconced between the North Sea and the fen
She failed to reproduce another child.

Sea captains find scant happiness ashore
And Nelson pestered vainly for command
His pleas ignored until exported war
Beyond the sea sent tremors through the land

While privately the more his body mined
So fruitlessly the more his love declined.

36   The fires of revolutionary France   *1792–3*
Flared, faded, flickered until Austria fanned
A patriotic blaze to check advance
By emigres and Brunswick. A demand

To soak French furrows in an impure blood
Inspired 'La Marseillaise'. Across the land
The human levees rose to curb the flood
And on the Valmy ridges made their stand.

Swift victory followed. France annexed Savoy
Pushed into Flanders and proclaimed its foes
To be all peoples who did not enjoy
A princeless regime. Liberty which grows

From wanton bloodshed is an evil thing.
The French in January killed their King.

SPANISH TRIUMPH & DISASTER

37   The hurried mustering before a war   *1793*
Now brought immediate posting to command
The speedy "Agamemnon", 64.
By fiat of Lord Chatham she was manned

By officers whom Nelson chose while men
From Norfolk volunteered. Three parsons brought
Their younger sons as hopeful midshipmen –
Both church and state despised the foe they fought.

Josiah Nisbet also went to sea
Apprenticed to his 'father's' deadly trade.
Once widowed Frances hid the truth that she
Of further loss was dreadfully afraid.

So went ambitious hope and older fears
To wars which lasted two and twenty years.

38   Down Channel "Agamemnon" went for Spain
And in Cadiz Hood's fleet was entertained
His squeamish captains jibbing at the pain
And slaughter of a bull fight. Unrestrained

And cruel bloodshed shocked these men of war.
Yet cheerfully when dined aboard the great
"Concepcion" all set but little store
On Spanish training, will-power or the state

Of discipline and said the six barge crews
From their small fleet could board and take by storm
This massive ship. Their hard professional views
Confirmed at sea when Spaniards failed to form

A practice battle line. Just four years on
John Jervis was to thrash the footling Don.

SPANISH TRIUMPH & DISASTER

39 By night off Naples soft sea zephyrs blow   1793
    And drifting scents which quit the land expire
    Where "Agamemnon" lay beneath the glow
    Vesuvius nurtures with its molten fire.

    Embayed in brightness under sun or moon
    Her captain to and from the palace went
    With Acton or with Hamilton and soon
    To Hood 6,000 local troops were sent.

    The handsome Hamilton had brains and zeal
    As Britain's envoy; sized his new guest's worth
    Deep called to deep in mutual appeal
    And friendship which survived a future birth

    To Emma Hamilton who learned the stress
    Two leading men put on an actoress.

40 The murderous Terror which possessed the French
    Affrighted Toulon and the southern coast.
    The port rebelled and barricade and trench
    Encircled it against a threatening host

    Of Jacobins from Paris. Hood sustained
    The siege until a Corsican appeared,
    A bitter man, in gunnery well trained
    Who stormed the headland which the Admiral feared

    Would dominate his ships. A bayonet thrust,
    Too low, pierced Buona Parte's thigh. Hood's fleet,
    Outgunned, burned enemies in dock. French lust
    For rebel blood filled gutters. The retreat

    Napoleon said showed fire upon the sea
    And blood on land in scarlet harmony.

SPANISH TRIUMPH & DISASTER

41   As war flared up a Paris sentence stilled   *1794*
The Austrian Emperor's daughter, France's Queen;
Brave chattering Marie Antoinette was killed –
Reginacide by plunging guillotine.

In other states the Terror fear inspired,
The dead queen's sister still in Naples reigned,
And British troops to Corsica retired
As Hood the blockade of Toulon maintained

While busy Nelson scurried port to port
Pursuing frigates, cutting off supplies
And landing troops and seamen to support
The island's independence. No surprise

Was possible and shots when under sail
Against stone frigates were of no avail.

42   The "Agamemnon's" crew fixed pulleys high
On ledges and walked downward hauling ropes
Which winched their ponderous cannon toward the sky
Then blasted starving Bastia down the slopes.

The foe clipped scouting Nelson in the back
And killed the guide and major at his side.
He criticised the troops for being slack
And lacking seamen's hardihood and pride.

When Bastia fell a garrison remained
At Calvi on the island's northern coast
And once again the Navy's guns were trained
From mountain sides where Nelson in a post

Was struck by debris and was backward tossed
His sight in one bruised eyeball being lost.

SPANISH TRIUMPH & DISASTER

43 Half blinded, bruised and cut, with ague's shakes,   *1794*
Its sweats redoubled by the July sun,
He stayed on duty, fired by will which makes
The frightened flesh outface the thundering gun

And wills to victory at whatever cost,
Inspires all smaller souls, yet also draws
New strength from men whose courage might be lost
Without beliefs in leaders and their cause.

To them he was devoted and refused
To transfer to a larger man o' war
While they no weakness in themselves excused
And strove to better all they did before.

Old "Agamemnons" showed rough humour when
They called themselves the "Eggs & Bacon" men.

44 The Admiralty stood down hook nosed Lord Hood,   *179.*
His senior captains, angry and distressed,
Swore that the change would bode no good
And Britain's fortunes locally regressed.

A scrambling fight, half battle, half pursuit
Left "Ca Ira" of 80 guns a prize
The "Agamemnon" luffing at acute
Far angles and bare half the other's size

Smashed in her stern and killed full half her crew
Ship handling and her gunnery supreme.
The cost but 13 hurt. In Nelson's view
The Admiral's recall signal killed the dream

That they might every French ship sink or take.
Hotham, said Hamilton, was not awake.

SPANISH TRIUMPH & DISASTER

45   So went affairs at sea while on the land   *1796*
Napoleon rushed the Austrians to defeat
Enthused and sparked his ragged shoeless band
And changed to rout the tempo of defeat.

For havering Hotham now came out Sir John
'Black Jack', 'Old Jarvie', harsh, near sixty three,
Hewn out, or born, at Stone, who slept upon
The deck and sold his bed when first at sea

To repay debt. He waged fierce war on those
Who minimised their service to the Crown.
He strove to rule and discipline impose
On slack commanders but the Jervis frown

Was tinged by humour and in Nelson's case
Each man saw eye to eye when face to face.

46   The Revolution boosted yet enslaved,
With 'Liberty' in Italy a toast;
In France Parisian followers, depraved,
In Notre Dame held high a whore as Host.

At Lodi's bridge and Monte Notte's height,
The gambler's rush, the unexpected hooks,
Put Piedmontese and Austrians to flight
And ripped the texts from military books.

And toppled kings and dukes as Buonaparte
From Lombardy to Tuscany moved on
And Naples, Rome and Corsica lost heart
And as they went so went the feckless Don

Who joined with France in making common war.
Nelson by then was rated Commodore.

SPANISH TRIUMPH & DISASTER

47   Now muddled Britain faced her numerous foes,   *1797*
Whose fleets from Texel to Toulon were spread,
With self-inflicted wounds that made her woes
Near mortal. There was ever present dread

Of Irish mayhem. Greedy and corrupt
Ill governance and Christian bigots gave
Good reason for both devious or abrupt
Plots or uprisings. Yet the Irish, brave

Beyond the normal, fought on sea and land
For Britain wrestling with an atheist foe.
Then starved, pay cheated seamen took a stand,
Red flagged in mutiny, yet swore to go

To sea if Spaniards, Dutch or French brought war
Near striking Spithead or the mutinous Nore.

48   The Cabinet, decisive in distress,
Abandoned Corsica, withdrew that fleet
West to Gibraltar. Nelson cursed the mess.
Evacuations and unfought defeat

Frustrated him. But old Sir John, more cool,
Knew island bases could not be sustained
Against both French and Spaniards. His strict rule
Drilled ships and seamen. Thus one fleet remained

In being cruising near the narrow strait.
Clean scrubbed, alert, decks sanded, rigging taut
And roamed beyond horizons as the fate
Of ill manned vessels languishing in port,

A distant noose of ships they never saw
Which slowly strangled allied men o' war.

John Jervis, Earl St Vincent

SPANISH TRIUMPH & DISASTER

49 Beyond Cadiz in morning calm and mist *14 Feb 179*
Two fleets converged upon an oily sea.
Sir John, south bound with fifteen ships, dismissed
All fear of Spanish numbers. "Let there be

Fifty and I'll go through them" he declared
As seven and twenty Spanish "thumpers loomed
Like Beachy Head in fog." Yet ill prepared
In twos and threes and clusters they were doomed

When sailing east downwind their straggling line
Was pierced by Jervis with the wind abeam
Which left adrift to lee their leading nine.
He wore and doubled back his well drilled team

Which ship by ship engaged the windward pack.
In "Captain" Nelson tried a different tack.

50 The Spanish, crowding sail, steered north to pass
Astern then eastward of the doubling line
To link their scattered vessels in a mass
Before their disarticulated spine

Was smashed in detail as the British brought
1200 guns to bear on half their fleet.
The Spaniards bore 1000 more yet fought
Half strength, with slower fire, and sought retreat

Which Nelson, sailing third from rear, divined,
Put up his helm and "Captain" headed back,
Toward "Santissima Trinidad" inclined
And fought her on the larboard tack,

The largest warship in the world which bore
Three score more guns than Nelson's seventy four.

SPANISH TRIUMPH & DISASTER

51 The Spanish four decked flagship, badly manned   *14 Feb 1797*
With only 80 seamen in her crew,
Bore near 1000 peasants from the land
Who knew not ropes, nor guns, nor what to do

In answer when the rapid broadsides crashed
From two decked "Captain" with "Culloden's" aid,
As flying timber splinters sliced and slashed
And heads and limbs and trunks were smashed and flayed.

See! Grey and acrid gouts of smoke enfold
In dingy fogs of war each ship and wave,
Ill lit by gun flash, by the west wind rolled
To shroud the charnel houses of the brave.

Wolf harried, herded sheep in pens abide –
Wind driven, lubbers' lumbering ships collide.

52 As "Excellent" came up her cannonade
Subdued two Spaniards, crippling a third,
"San Nicolas" of 80 guns, and made
Her luff into "San Josef" in absurd

Embranglements of rigging, spars and mast.
The sail ripped "Captain" carefully was laid
Aboard the first ship's quarter drifting past.
A crunch of timbers and a rush was made

By seamen, soldiers and three midshipmen
Who burst the gallery window and its door,
Shot startled officers on deck and then,
The colours down, bruised Nelson to the fore

Received surrendered swords but fire again
From aft on "San Josef" dropped seven men.

SPANISH TRIUMPH & DISASTER

53   Marines above companionways were placed   *14 Feb 1797*
        To keep the crew below. At Nelson's bawl
        To Miller in the "Captain" more men raced
        And climbed or swung aboard to rush the tall

        "San Josef" from "San Nicolas" and take
        A Spaniard from a Spanish deck. Now burned
        His incandescent 'orb' and for its sake
        He banished fear and fatal danger spurned.

        His chosen role to play the hero made
        Him act in action as he'd cast his part,
        The gallant actor who obeyed and played
        The script on which he set, and risked, his heart.

        "The Abbey or to victory!" he cried
        Ensuring drama if he lived or died.

54   Across the great ship's mainchains Berry hauled
        His Commodore amid the drifting smoke
        As from the quarter deck a Spaniard called
        "We yield", his Admiral dying as he spoke.

        The courtly Captain bent his knee and gave
        His sword to Nelson who was ringed by men
        Who'd served in "Agamemnon". All were brave
        By nature but their inspiration then

        Was selfless leadership whose selfish aim
        Was self fulfilment by performing such
        Great services as lead to earthly fame,
        Embellished with the kindly Nelson touch.

        His bargeman, William Fearney, strong and calm
        Bundled surrendered swords beneath his arm.

SPANISH TRIUMPH & DISASTER

55   The dusk advanced behind St Vincent's Cape,   *14 Feb 1797*
Four captured warships flew the Union Jack
And hammered Spaniards hurried to escape
To shelter in Cadiz. The chase turned back

To jury rig its masts, re-reeve its ropes
As Nelson by his Admiral was received
With open arms in "Victory". All the hopes
Of victory which the allies had conceived

Were smoke upon a skyline. Now Toulon
Cadiz, Ferrol, Boulogne, Den Helder, Brest,
Could not combine their fleets. This battle won
To thwart invasion left bizarrely dressed

Nelson, hat shot, cut clothing near obscene
And Jervis spattered with a dead marine.

56   A nation's praise, awards, a king's acclaim
Flowed forth at once to match the butcher's bill
His ship's two dozen dead brought Nelson fame
And six and fifty hurt let "Captain" fill

The post of "honour" in a fleet which lost
Three hundred casualties, a quarter killed;
As blood is reckoned but a little cost
To pay for national strategy fulfilled.

The losses in the shattered Spanish fleet
Were heavier but far below the toll
Of war on land in victory or defeat
Yet yielded all the narrow seas control

To Nelson with a knighthood to his name
And Earl St Vincent, as Sir John became.

SPANISH TRIUMPH & DISASTER

57   St Vincent grimly ordered close blockade   *1797*
Of Cadiz and sent Nelson's ships inshore
To sap the strength of Spain by cannonade
And occupy arrivals from the Nore,

So lately mutinous, with savage war
Of boats and batteries, sword on sword,
The slash of cutlass and the swing of oar
The strokes to lift a crew aboard

Felucca, brig or ketch and take a prize,
The Navy's carrot – payment for success.
Its stick a Captain's power to authorise
A nine lash flogging, often to excess.

St Vincent once resorted to the use,
One Sunday, of the yardarm and the noose.

58   The rhythmic motions of an anchored ship
In springtime by a darkening Spanish shore
Slid tabled charts with every rise and dip
Swung light on weathered faces plotting war.

Half lit, strong features, concentrating, tanned,
Outlined as shadows on the cabin wall;
Sea sounds without; and quiet talk which planned
To aid their country but enrich them all.

Fremantle, Troubridge, Miller, Waller heard
Rear Admiral Nelson plotting this attack
By night on Santa Cruz, all undeterred
By scanty information and the lack

Of ship borne troops. No fears of a defeat
Outweighed chimeras of a treasure fleet.

SPANISH TRIUMPH & DISASTER

59   Premonitory scratchings with his quill   1797
      By Thorp in "Terpischore" the previous night
      Detailed his assets and set down his will;
      Consoled his parents that the coming fight

      Would prove their son had faithful duty done.
      The veteran Captain Bowen eased his plight
      With hope of pension once the town was won.
      Each heard the surf on rocks at dead of night

      Beneath the pyramid of Tenerife
      As boat crews strained against the wind and rain
      Their will and strength sustained by false belief
      In Spanish weakness and of easy gain.

      From ambush cannon blast and musket volley
      Along the mole took sanguine toll for folley.

60   Hunched from their boats and bunched upon the quay
      The "Theseus" party met the hissing grape
      Which scythed them down betwixt the stone and sea.
      Some crawled or stumbled, bloodied, to escape

      To rocking boats half sheltered by the wall.
      For Nelson, Walpole sword just drawn, the blow
      Smashed elbow bones. His left hand at his fall
      Reclutched the sword. He knew one arm must go.

      His stepson found him and began to staunch
      The flowing blood with an arterial grip,
      Half dragged the failing Admiral to a launch
      And set the seamen pulling for the ship.

      The "Fox" sank then and Nelson paused to make
      His oarsmen save the few their boat could take.

SPANISH TRIUMPH & DISASTER

61   The full boat wallowing in the driving rain   1797
Neared "Seahorse" but he would not go aboard
For fear the sight should cause much needless pain
To new wed Betsy Wynne who so adored

Her Captain Fremantle whose fate ashore
None knew amidst the darkness and the storm;
"Sir, you may die if we expose you more."
"Then die I will," replied the sea cloaked form

Upon the bottom boards. The crew tugged on
And gained the lee of "Theseus" but their call
For bosun's chair was checked. "I still have one
Good arm. And legs." He climbed the wooden wall

A rope in his left hand and caused alarm
With "Tell the surgeon I must lose my arm."

62   A swig of rum, the wad for teeth to clench
Then, pinioned by two hefty surgeon's mates,
He sensed the severing knife sweeps' cold; a French
Expletive from the royalist surgeon; grates

Of saw on bone. Arm off. Short stump. "My fin."
He, mocking, called it when the wound was healed.
In ill-lit haste a nerve was trapped within
The suterings as "Theseus" pitched and reeled.

"Shall we preserve your arm, Sir?" "No. Just throw
It in the hammock with the man who died
Beside me." Useless now. So let it go
Into the pointless past with wind and tide.

The future mattered. Lured by its demands
In half an hour he issued fresh commands.

SPANISH TRIUMPH & DISASTER

63   In Santa Cruz swift peace succeeded war   *1797*
The hurt were tended and the prisoners fed.
And British ships allowed to send ashore
To ferry off the captives and their dead.

The generous Spanish Governor arranged
For boats' crews drink and biscuits and to end
Hostilities casked wine for ale exchanged;
The foe of yesterday the morrow's friend.

And Nelson with a graciousness to match
This kindness sought despite his pain
The privilege of bearing the despatch
On his defeat the Governor sent to Spain.

His outward calm and firmness all impressed.
But inward secondary shock depressed.

64   The anodyne of action calmed his nerve
Left handed letters trickled from his pen
A "mutilated carcase" could not serve,
He feared, his country or his King again.

The deaths of Bowen, Thorp and twelve score more
All troubled him. Dramatically he felt
His fate a pensioner both maimed and poor
Who in a "hut" or "humble cottage" dwelt.

So early letters ran. Self-pitying grief
Was conquered in three weeks for when he dined
Aboard St Vincent's flagship a belief
In future services possessed his mind.

His Admiral said he would again request
His posting and all marvelled at his zest.

SPANISH TRIUMPH & DISASTER

65   The steady English hold hard minded views   *1797*
On war, regarding victory or defeat
As incidents. The raid at Santa Cruz
A mere misfortune for a gallant fleet.

Inured to shipping sunk and seamen lost
The news from Tenerife where many died
Was stoically received, the human cost
Accepted with the comment "Well, they tried."

For courage, boldness, judgement were three traits
The nation measured men by. All success
Resulted from their use and public praise
Went to the first two; judgement mattered less.

Thus Nelson homeward as a hero came
A limb deducted but with added fame.

66   His stump, to which St Vincent, jesting, "bowed"
For months was painful, partly healed, inflamed.
His wife, in Bath and London humbly proud,
Each day applied a dressing but was shamed

To own distaste. She had good cause to weep,
He paid her duty but his ardent heart
Was with his Service. Opium brought him sleep
From throbbing pain yet still he sought a part

In those great dramas on the distant seas
Which fashioned history and spread English speech
And British genes across the world. His pleas
To Admiralty, when fit, were heard. The beach

No place for Nelson when all Europe saw
Triumphant France prepared for conquering war.

THE BAND OF BROTHERS

1798

THE BAND OF BROTHERS

67   Le Directoire in Paris coldly eyed   *1798*
Their one unbeaten enemy and planned
A major expedition to decide
The contest where their ships need not command

The narrow seas to let French troops invade
A prosperous England for, said Buonaparte
In Picardy, "That voyage can not be made."
And on an Eastern Empire set his heart.

To conquer Egypt would create the chance
To aid the Sultan in far off Mysore
Switch Britain's Indian trade to France
Awe Europe and bring wealth from distant war.

A plan for life beneath the tyrants' rods
Who were, the Royal Navy proved, not gods.

68   From whence to where and when and in what strength
Would France strike forth? The answers were unknown
In London but, inevitably, at length
Good guesstimates were made. The wind had blown

Nelson by then in "Vanguard" down to Spain
And old St Vincent prowling off the Straits.
To wait for news of French intent was vain,
For who wastes time in war capitulates

Allowing enemies to work their will.
"With three large ships and frigates as your eyes
Cruise to the east" St Vincent said "until
You learn their purpose. Then cut off supplies."

The Admiralty's conclusions were the same.
An extra squadron to Gibraltar came.

THE BAND OF BROTHERS

69   Pitt with Dundas and Spencer gave much thought   *1798*
To strategy and Cabinet assent
At length was given after Pitt had sought
Consent to an offensive. Ships were sent

From Irish coasts and from the Channel Fleet
To blockade western ports in France and Spain.
They joined by night and practised a deceit,
Assuming markings which before were plain

To telescopes upon the Spanish shore,
On other vessels covertly withdrawn
To form a squadron which could change the war,
With fear of French invasion turned to scorn.

As Buonaparte said after his eclipse,
"Whichever way I turned I found your ships."

70   The instant reinforcing tops'ls rose
Upon St Vincent's skyline he despatched
Ten major ships to Nelson. Those he chose
The best in his blockading fleet. Unmatched

Were "Culloden" with Troubridge and the tall
Canadian Hallowell in "Swiftsure". Gould
"Audacious" led. For Eastern conquests Ball
Advanced with "Alexander". Saumarez ruled

"Orion" with volunteers and no pressed crew,
Most from his native Guernsey. "Minotaur"
Had Thomas Louis in command who drew
His name from French royal forebears. He made war

As ruthlessly on France as all the others
Who gathered now as Nelson's Band of Brothers.

THE BAND OF BROTHERS

71   "Bellerophon" had Darby in command,   *1798*
The 'Billy Ruffian' of the seamen's slang;
The sails of "Theseus" felt a Miller's hand
And Thompson called the tune "Leander" sang.

"Goliath" had Foley and the "Zealous" Hood,
Peyton "Defence" and Hardy small "Mutine".
"Majestic" Westcott bore. All eastward stood
Befogged between 'May be' and 'May have been'.

The west wind whistled 'Enemies to lee.'
Yet where, whence, how, how many, to what end?
No answers showed upon that empty sea
Swept clear, by fear, of neutral, foe or friend.

To dine and talk of tactics captains went
Each day to "Vanguard", hounds without a scent.

72   Their huntsman and their mentor now possessed
A copy of the Admiralty's command
To smash the Toulon fleet, which also stressed
He held the fate of Europe in his hand.

And gave him further liberty to rove
Through Hellespont to Euxine in his quest.
He answered Spencer, saying that he strove
To find the French. His squadron would not rest

Until successful, even if their course
Was to Australia. A passing sail
Said France had conquered Malta with a force
Of 40,000 troops. The skipper's tale

That near 400 transports journeyed on
Anticipated truths they acted on.

THE BAND OF BROTHERS

73   Lord Spencer at the Admiralty received   *1798*
       A second Nelson letter. "I believe
       If they pass Sicily a plan conceived
       With Tipoo in South India to retrieve

       Their mutual fortunes has been put in hand."
       Possessing Alexandria was the key
       For through that port across Egyptian sand
       French force could flow to Indian victory.

       With crowded sail across a summer sea
       He hurried on not knowing that his prey
       Sailed half a day astern in jeopardy.
       One night they neared but Brueys swung away

       His giant convoy in alarm, deterred
       When distant British signal guns were heard.

74   A fevered Nelson made futile pursuit
       Of foes now falling further still astern
       As lack of frigates caused his fleet acute
       Frustration, for no look-out could discern

       More than the hot horizon, empty, blue
       Where sky and sea merged colours and in turn
       Were tinged by shadows of a distant few
       White cloudlets and the wings of gull or tern.

       Yet decks were kept as clear as sky of cloud
       And crews on guns were daily exercised
       Or drilled at seamanship and musketry. Allowed
       Five minutes for three broadsides. Realised

       Such concentrated shot must overwhelm
       A ship's crew, cannon, all three masts and helm.

THE BAND OF BROTHERS

75   So, hurriedly, to Egypt Nelson came.   *1798*
Its coast was clear and in the seedy port
To which a Grecian conqueror gave his name
A Turkish man-of-war transferred support

To troops on land. Its guns were sent ashore
As British ships swept north, a blind man's chase
To Syria and Crete four hours before
The French appeared. The tortoise won that race.

And Nelson, all impetuosity
And ardent bravery personified,
Might well have killed Napoleon at sea
If patience had his courage modified

Or cunning cooled his incandescent core
And so saved Europe seventeen years of war.

76   The British squadron's urgent diligence
Swung them to Sicily. In Syracuse
While watering ships there came intelligence –
"No French to westward." Nelson at the news

Raced for the isles of Greece and heard from Turks
A great fleet steered, four weeks before, south east.
"The devil's children do the devil's works
And have the devil's luck" he wrote. At least

He knew which way the devil lay and drove
Towards the Levant and still the daily drills
Perfected gunnery and still they strove
To polish seamanship and killing skills.

To overwhelm a part by all combined
Each captain knew was in his Admiral's mind.

THE BAND OF BROTHERS

77   Four weeks ashore, with savants in his train   1798
      To document his triumphs and record
      Egyptian ancient wonders and explain
      The plundered treasures which he took abroad,

      Left Buonaparte victorious on the sand.
      "Some 40 centuries look down" he cried
      As Ottoman defenders made their stand
      Beside the Pyramids. Massed guns, he spied,

      Upon one flank lacked carriages. He pushed
      Against the other and his squares impaled
      Or shot the Mamelukes whose horses rushed
      Upon them in attacks which always failed.

      On land fire power and discipline prevail.
      To sea the bloodied Nile conveyed that tale.

78   Once more unto the low and sandy line   1 Aug 1798
      Of Egypt's coast the British squadron steered
      And sought through jiggling heat haze to define
      As yards or masts such straightness as appeared

      Against the sky above a turquoise sea.
      A tricolour told Alexandria's tale
      Of occupation by an enemy
      Whose fleet had sailed. Eyes strained against the pale

      Horizon's glare that August afternoon.
      The birds had flown. Each captain took it hard,
      Saumarez "was near despondency"; yet soon
      Young Eliot from "Goliath's" royal yard

      Slid down the back-stay, raced the deck and said
      "Thirteen of the line, four frigates lie ahead!"

THE BAND OF BROTHERS

79   Without formation change the British steered   *1 Aug 1798*
Straight for the anchored French with double shot
In loaded cannon; decks already cleared;
Spare sails tight rolled and soaked to stop the hot

Outspray of sparks or embers spreading fire.
French ships shore hugging in a crescent lay,
A shallow sickle shaped to give entire
Sandbank and shoal protection in the Bay

Of Aboukir, each anchored by the head.
De Brueys believed with batteries on land
His anchorage safe. The British swung the lead
And called the fathoms near the outer sand

With space, as Foley in "Goliath" saw,
Where foes could swing for friends to pass inshore.

80   "Engage the van and centre." Nelson flew
Few other signals as his squadron closed;
His friends, each vessel's captain, knew
His plan for anchored vessels so disposed.

Approach from windward and allow the lee
Division of self-tethered ships to see,
Transfixed in helpless immobility,
Disaster gliding from the open sea.

And owl-like as the daylight dimmed
Wings spread to catch an evening air
The floating white sails of the British trimmed
Across the sunset and brave Frenchmen there

Knew death was drifting down that gentle breeze
Which moved the ruthless masters of the seas.

Thomas Foley

THE BAND OF BROTHERS

81 Hood in the "Zealous" hailed to lead the way. *1 Aug 1798*
From "Vanguard" Nelson doffed to give him leave
But Foley swung "Goliath" into play
To shuttle where foes thought no ship could weave

Round "Guerrier" the leading seventy four
Progressing down the larboard of their line
Betwixt the anchored warships and the shore
Where on that side their ill trained crews, supine,

Had lower gun ports closed and lumber piled
Upon the deck. The frigate "Serieuse" tried
To stop his passage. Foley, tense and riled
Called "Sink that brute!" "Goliath", each broadside

Erupting, came to anchor having wrought
A sinking starboard, a dismasting port.

82 "Orion" and "Zealous" followed Foley through
With "Theseus" and "Audacious" close astern,
The British line of battle forked in two
Round "Guerrier" and "Conquerant" to earn

That pair's surrender when their masts were gone
And rigging, yards and canvas draped their wrecks
Encumbering ports. Dead French were heaped upon
Shot furrowed, splintered, scored and bloodied decks.

Then "Vanguard" wafted from the sinking day's
Red death-bed underneath an orange sun's
Descent illumined by its golden rays
Assailed the silent dusk with all her guns.

Out thought, out fought, attacked on either side
The next French ships with starboard guns replied.

THE BAND OF BROTHERS

83   The "Vanguard" anchored by the "Spartiate"   1 Aug 1798
And poured in cross-fire. Seven British ships
Now clustered round three French whose bloody fate
Their gallantry prolonged. The swift eclipse

Of "Peuple Souverain" sprang from a ball
Which sheered her anchor cable and allowed
Escape by drift from gunshot but the tall
Unhandy ship was wrecked, the sand her shroud.

And langridge, scrap iron, fired to slash a sail
Or sever British ropes, clipped Nelson's brow,
A blood warm flap of skin dropped down, a veil
Across his "bright" eye as he called that now

The French had killed him. He despaired of life
And begged to be remembered to his wife.

84   The sailing master of "Bellerophon"
Misjudged her anchoring distance and sailed on
Beneath the towering bulk of "L'Orient".
Within the hour the Briton's masts were gone,

The "Ruffian", Darby wounded, drifted free
Unlit in darkness. "Swiftsure" proved her name
As Hallowell arrived but could not see
Which ship she was and held his fire yet came

Quick to her anchorage and renewed her fight
Against the flagship of 120 guns.
His 74 hard hammered her as light
Grew on her deck and then replaced the sun's.

Fresh paint and new tarred rigging fed the fire –
An Admiral's three decked ship his funeral pyre.

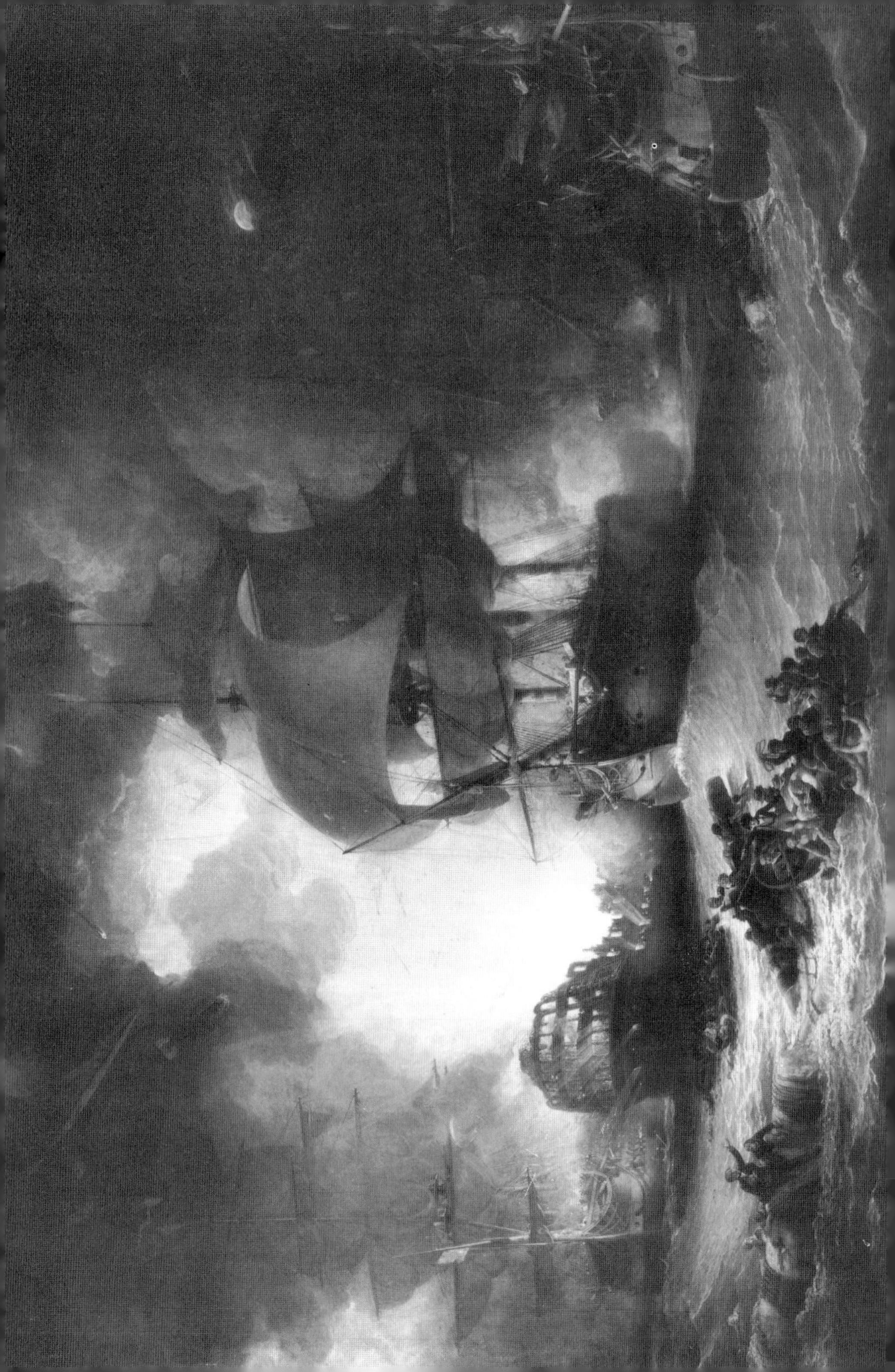

THE BAND OF BROTHERS

85 Across the berth of "Peuple Souverain" *1 Aug 1798*
   Swam 50 gun "Leander" where she swung
   To anchor as her batteries began
   Along the line a raking fire which stung

   Both "L'Orient" and "Franklin" all their length
   While they from tapered bows with shattered crews
   Could not repay such punishment. French strength
   Was ebbing fast when Berry gave the news

   Of "L'Orient's" fire to Nelson who arose,
   Head bandaged, went on deck and saw the spires
   Of golden flame creep up her masts, their glows
   Contrasting with that disc of silver fires

   A moon in Egypt shining on the sand
   Reflected from both water and the land.

86 Men knew disaster loomed. They saw the blaze
   Spread on the biggest ship in either fleet
   And limelight vessels through the smoke and haze
   Of expired broadsides. Britons, quick to meet

   New dangers, sluiced their decks, wet rigging, closed
   Their gunports and secured each magazine.
   The French veered cables and all crews exposed
   To "L'Orient's" glare were audience to a scene

   Where centre stage the burning grand pariah
   Was shunned by all. De Brueys, now dying, chose
   His deck to lie on. "A French Admiral must expire
   Upon his quarter deck." A deck which rose

   A hundred feet in splinters when at last
   His ship disintegrated in the blast.

THE BAND OF BROTHERS

87   The silence of the desert cloaked the sound   *1/2 Aug 1798*
As skies rained embers, masts and mangled men
While distant Muslims sensed the trembling ground
Portended victory and peace again.

On every ship shocked seamen ceased to fight
And Nelson sent his one sound boat to save
The few who lived; the soft Egyptian night
An instant shroud for those who lacked a grave.

And jaded British sailors dropped asleep
Incontinently by their guns and lay
In awkward twos and threes until the peep
Of dawnlight flushed and swilled the night away.

The British down the static line moved on
For conquests past the vanished "L'Orient".

88   "Heureux", "Mercure", "Tonnant" and "Artemise"
Were shortly overcome. Five others fled
At Villeneuve's command to open seas
But Miller in the "Theseus" quickly read

The French intent and "Timoleon" bore
The damage of his broadsides and was lost
When, faute de mieux, she ran herself ashore
The thirteenth vessel which the battle cost

Defeated France besides five thousand men
Taken or dead. The British found each prize
A charnel house, for Catholic widows then
Had need of witnesses to authorise

Remarriage later. But when Britons died
Their shipmates swiftly pitched them overside.

THE BAND OF BROTHERS

89   "A conquest, not a victory." Nelson said.   1798
A just description of results which flowed
From boldness, teamwork and the sloven dead.
Without a screen of frigates Brueys rode

At anchor and was taken unaware
By Nelson's coming and had flimsy sheds,
Troops dormitories, on decks still standing where
Toulon had fixed them. Thence the deadly shreds

Of flying woodwork rent by British shot
Scythed all his decks or stoked the "L'Orient's" flame.
Hence Buonaparte, who strove to cure the rot
Of Ottoman misgovernment, became,

Despite his power, by sea and sand confined,
A conqueror and prisoner combined.

90   Reaction follows action and the strain
Of constant search and exercise of will
To chase a foe and face his fire again
Then grapple until conquest or the kill

Left Nelson shaken with a throbbing brain.
Six score and four engagements under fire
An eye and arm destroyed and now the pain
Of "splitting, splitting" headaches and entire

Blindness in spells and every third day stain
Of sweat on clothes as fevers surging higher,
Malarial tertians, fluxed. The steady drain
Of energy and strength he said was dire.

His flagship sailed towards Naples. Gusting blasts
Blew men away and snapped her jib and masts.

A FOREIGN COURT

1798–1800

A FOREIGN COURT

91 As damaged "Vanguard" moved across the bay *1798*
Musicians from the opera house began
A sea-borne "Rule Britannia", then to play
Both nations' anthems when the festive plan

The palace and the embassy contrived
Unfolded. In salute the cannons roared
As myriad escorts and his barge arrived
Beside the flagship with the King aboard.

But first, before the portly Ferdinand
Was welcomed, Lady Hamilton bedecked
With naval favours entered as she planned
Dramatically, spread out her arms, then checked

Wide eyed. "Oh God! Is't possible?" she cried
And swooned upon her hero's unmaimed side.

92 Heroic Nelson was for months attacked
With flattery and praise and all her art
By Emma Hamilton who never lacked
Ambition or the skill to play a part

In politics and use her husband's place
To help the Court of Naples and its Queen.
Robust and statuesque. A radiant face.
A Cheshire blacksmith's daughter. She had been

A happy, zestful mistress at sixteen
Then carefully trained to sing and dance and act.
Her classic *attitudes plastiques* were seen
By all with awe. Her sympathy and tact,

Her common sense and courage and support
Made Britain's envoy's wife a friend at court.

A FOREIGN COURT

93 Yet Emma had her past to overcome. 1798
    Adopted by a Greville as his tart
    Then passed on to his uncle for a sum
    That cleared his debts but did not switch her heart.

    That uncle, William Hamilton, was kind,
    An ex-Guardee, sophisticated, brave,
    Ambassador to Naples, with a mind
    Informed and sharp. A generous man who gave

    Collections of antiquities and art
    To Britain and whom Emma later wed.
    Her friendship with the Queen had played its part
    In victualling Nelson's squadron it was said

    In Syracuse. It needed women's guile
    To break neutrality before the Nile.

94 Maria Carolina who was born
    To Austria's ruler and whose sister died
    Beneath the guillotine, was always torn
    Between her fears of murder and her pride.

    This Queen in southern Italy relied
    Upon the strength and country common sense
    Of Lady Hamilton. Her King denied
    His subjects freedom but sought English pence

    And ships and Austrian troops to clear the land
    Of occupying French but Austria failed
    To send support and portly Ferdinand
    With Marshal Mack led local troops who quailed.

    A comic opera armament which ran
    The instant drummers tapped the *rataplan*.

A FOREIGN COURT

95 Although the Neapolitans reached Rome, 1798
    Quite unopposed their progress ended when
    French garrisons moved south. They fled for home,
    From 19,000 losing 40 men.

    And Nelson, recently entitled Lord,
    Knew monarch and his ministers and court
    Would in their panic seek to swarm aboard
    His transports and his warships off the port

    When enemies arrived and turncoats changed
    Allegiance to a Jacobin regime.
    He quietly with the Hamiltons arranged
    A refugee evacuation scheme.

    In holds offshore where waiting shipping rode
    Royal treasures worth three million pounds were stowed.

96 A mid-December night of on-shore gales,
    Of bitter, gusting winds and lopping seas,
    Of weary pulls to ships with stricken sails
    Then dangerous boardings in their rolling lees

    Brought passengers to "Vanguard" in their flight
    To Sicily and safety who were all
    Spray soaked and trembling, paralysed by fright.
    The wind blew harder than he could recall,

    Wrote Nelson, at a time before, or since,
    When Emma sacrificed her sheets and bed
    To royal children, cradling one prince
    Against her breast twelve hours 'til he was dead

    While six years old Alberto's parents lay
    In prayer and terror through that Christmas Day.

A FOREIGN COURT

97 Sea power, that flexible yet puissant force, *1798–9*
 From Picardy turned Buonaparte away
 And now by water's fluid strength his course
 Was changed again as ships to guard Bombay,

 Not needed after Aboukir, withdrew
 From Bab-el-Mandeb and the Arabian Sea;
 The Russians and the Turks relieved Corfu
 From French invaders and the tyranny

 In looted Malta eased when Portuguese
 And British ships appeared. Persistent Pitt
 Raised up a coalition with more ease
 When flames from "L'Orient" freedom's torch had lit.

 All Europe was inclined to make a stand
 When Buonaparte was stranded in the sand.

98 To burst that bond he marched 10,000 north,
 Stormed Jaffa, capturing 2,000 Turks,
 Then short of food and water, drove them forth,
 Unarmed, and murdered all. The devil lurks

 Within all men with arbitrary powers
 Whose actions may be chronicled on stones
 Or celebrated with bay wreaths and flowers –
 Or marked by heaps of desert whitened bones.

 Through Turkey and through Austria to France
 He told his staff their troops would march, a boast
 Nemesis met, confining them to dance,
 A locust plague, upon the Syrian coast

 As once again the Royal Navy came
 To douse the glim of this cold killer's fame.

A FOREIGN COURT

99 A lack of tractive power and roads for wheels   1799
    Forced Buonaparte to move his guns by sea,
    Supply and transport two Achilles heels
    Which stopped the conqueror from breaking free

    Of Egypt, vengeful Turks and naval grip.
    Sir Sidney Smith with both his 74s,
    The "Tigre" and "Theseus", took each coastal ship
    Which bore French ammunition, guns and stores.

    The fort at Acre on the coast road stopped
    The French advance and frenzied storming failed
    To carry the Crusader fort and lopped
    The aliens' ranks as British vessels sailed

    Close in, their gunfire flashing in support
    Of captured cannon landed through the port.

100 Smith led his seamen and marines ashore,
    A stiffening to the hard pressed Turks' defence,
    And held attacks on breach and tower before
    The glory seeking Buonaparte saw sense

    And left his piles of dead. His pharmacist
    Brought no medicaments but camel loads
    Of wine to sell to wounded troops whose tryst
    With death was yet to come on dusty roads

    Southbound to Egypt from the plague, the heat,
    From dysentery or circling Turks. Smith's stand
    And Turkish sea-borne troops forced French retreat,
    Rehearsal for the Russian snows in sand.

    "Smith made me miss my destiny", so said
    Napoleon, heedless of the needless dead.

A FOREIGN COURT

101 The flaws of diamonds are exposed by light *1798*
And pressures mould those gemstones in the rock;
So character is formed by every fight
If men endure and overcome the shock

Of war and tides of enervating fear.
Yet diamonds into graphite may be turned,
As faults in men more readily appear,
When inner cores electrically are burned

Or soothing flattery flows into ears
To melt resolve and bubble-up self-love.
A Siren flatterer her victim steers,
An eagle convoyed by a conquering dove

Towards shipwreck. Nelson now was so obsessed
By Emma that his captains were distressed.

102 The Band of Brothers serving at the Nile
Lost Westcott there and an explosion aft
Killed Miller with some "Theseus" seamen while
Bombarding Acre. Nelson felt that shaft

Of fate and, lonely, from his flagship wrote
Of "Poor, dear Miller ... much lamented friend".
With Berry sick ashore those still afloat
Dispersed to other waters and the end

Of Nelson's area independence loomed
When sick St Vincent yielded post to Keith;
Tired tetchiness and infringed pride presumed
The Scot a man he should not serve beneath.

Good actors aping courage conquer hell –
Until sick bodies and tired minds rebel.

A FOREIGN COURT

103   Good reason for his ardent wish to keep   1799
      Close links with Emma at the Naples Court
      Came with "The Army of the Faith" whose deep
      Revulsion at French theft and rapine brought

      Ruffo's banditti surging to the sea
      Across Calabria and the Appenines
      When fierce Italian longing to be free
      Of godless foreign soldiers straightened spines

      And stiffened wills of peasantry who fled
      With poltroon officers the year before.
      Their occupiers were besieged instead
      And gladly signed good terms to end the war

      Which Ruffo offered. "Vanguard" crossed the Bay
      And Nelson vetoed everything next day.

104   As Suvarov and Russian troops marched west
      In northern Italy to Austria's aid
      In Rome and Naples those who thought their best
      Way forward was with France were now afraid

      For from the Po French garrisons withdrew
      And sea lanes were by British ships controlled
      Scant refuge now for Jacobins who flew;
      For captives noose or cell and none parolled.

      Caracciolo who was British trained
      Until the Court's flight led his King's fleet well;
      French death threats turned his loyalty he explained
      When dragged in rags from hiding in a well.

      Authoritarian Nelson sought a trial
      For mutiny and treason he deemed vile.

A FOREIGN COURT

105   A Naples naval court convened in haste   *1799*
Judged instant death the proper punishment
As Nelson urged that there should be no waste
Of time upon appeals. His fierce intent

To crush revolt surmounted native sloth.
Caracciolo by that sunset swung
Beneath a Naples yardarm. Then with both
Feet lashed to double shot the corpse was flung

Into the blue Tyrrhenian Sea. A breeze,
When gasses filled the stomach, blew it back
Upright towards harbour bobbing through the seas.
The frightened King, upon a mental rack,

Was calmed on hearing Hamilton surmise
"His conscience brings him to apologise."

106   The presents and the honours which had flowed
To Nelson from the Turks and other courts
Were capped by Naples when the King bestowed
A Dukedom on him. Subsequent reports

Of Bronte on its scrubby hillside showed
Decay and ruin spreading over all
That flaking hamlet. Yet with pride he glowed
And letters with both titles signed. The tall

Canadian Hallowell who shipped a mast
At Aboukir from "L'Orient" with it gave
His Admiral a hint that at the last
"The paths of glory lead but to the grave",

For Nelson on the "Vanguard's" hatch was laid
A coffin "Swiftsure's" carpenter had made.

A FOREIGN COURT

107   As Ball blockaded Malta Troubridge moved   *1799*
On Capua and sent picked men ashore
To cannonade the French, a step which proved
Enough to force surrender. "Minotaur"

With Louis off the Tiber threatened Rome
Which yielded when his barge was rowed upstream.
As Nelson told St Vincent, now at home,
To clear the French from Italy would seem

A greater service than to heed Lord Keith
Who ordered concentration to defend
Majorca. Nelson disobeyed his chief
And kept the ships he ordered him to send.

His judgement proved correct yet strict Whitehall
Sent reprimands and Hamilton's recall.

108   French troops beseiged in Malta were reduced   *1800*
To eating rats but Ball lacked troops to storm
Valetta's fort. His courtesy induced
Devotion from the Maltese but their warm

Regard was tempered by starvation's chill.
Ball's pleas to buy from Naples were rebuffed
Despite Sicilian granaries' overspill.
The "Alexander's" first lieutenant bluffed

Officials in Girgenti; from that port
Brought laden corn ships out and promptly paid
Delighted owners for the grain he bought.
Complaints were by unbribed officials laid.

But Britain told the King all knew he would
Approve this action for the general good.

A FOREIGN COURT

109   The new "Foudroyant", fresh from England, flew   *1800*
The flag of Nelson when the French essayed
To run supplies to Malta and renew
Their garrison beset by the blockade.

Implacably the Royal Navy closed
Upon the convoy and the small "Success"
With 32 light guns herself imposed
Across the course of "Genereux" whose press

Of canvas was reduced when careful fire
Ripped off her stay sails, slowed the 74,
Struck down her Admiral, left him to expire
Before "Foudroyant" and "Audacious" bore

Alongside with "Northumberland" to claim
The prize resulting from the frigate's aim.

110   When "Genereux" gave up, 2,000 men
Aboard a trooper and two storeships fell
To Nelson's frigates. His left handed pen
With spidery scratches was employed to tell

Lord Minto London thought he was unfit
To have the area's overall command.
What better right had Keith to merit it?
It took Nelsonic nous to understand

That Perree in the "Genereux" would take
His vessels southward to the Barbary coast
And plot which intercepting course to make
The Frenchman's dash disastrous. Nelson's boast,

"Four Admirals and nineteen of the line
I've seen submit." He threatened to resign.

A FOREIGN COURT

111   His correspondence now showed much distress   *1800*
At what he felt was Admiralty neglect,
Deliberately contrived, of his success.
As faithful dogs which bring the kill expect

A pat upon the head so Nelson yearned
For overall command. A nervous fret
Possessed him when he felt that what he'd earned
Was still withheld. He wrote then in a pet,

Self pityingly of quitting through ill health
Tormenting him. Seasickness, aching teeth,
Headaches, a running eye. He feared the stealth
Of creeping blindness. Nervously beneath

These symptoms showing that he should depart
Was the disorder of a shaking heart.

112   A palpitation in an aching breast
Brought on by strain and hardship and the lack
Of leave to England, happiness or rest.
He knew his Nisbet step-son faced the sack,

A brave post-Captain, yet unruled and spoiled,
For whose advancement Nelson always spoke
Or wrote to seniors but whose conduct roiled
Relationships. "I fear he must be broke."

A childless Admiral told his distant wife.
He took the Hamiltons to view the war
Off Malta as the April sun brought life
And warmth with Spring. Behind the cabin door

With love and passion Emma met his need
And willing pulchritude took in his seed.

A FOREIGN COURT

113 His captains hoped he would remain at sea 1800
Until the capture of the "Guillaume Tell"
Close watched in Malta. He ignored their plea
Yet when that Aboukir survivor fell

To Berry, he effulgently described
His absence as a happiness. It gave
His "children" glory which would be ascribed
To them alone. To some who risk the grave

Before their natural time such glory counts
Far more than pay. The honours which they crave
They seek from native or from foreign founts
To signify and prove that they were brave.

The guidance of his "orb" controlled his story
And Nelson gloried therefore in his glory.

114 Not all courageous men approved his stance.
That stern Glaswegian, Major General Moore,
Eight years before Corunna, at a glance
Surmised his state and wrote he cut so poor

"And pitiful a figure; brave, good man"
When Hamiltons attended on the Queen
And he on Emma as all four began
To travel North from Leghorn. Moore had seen

The ribbons, stars and medals on his coat
Whereof the cloth was covered by the blaze
Of Turkish baubles. That, Moore thought, remote
From "Nelson, Conqueror of the Nile", whose bays

Though "well deserved" worn daily showed a folly
"A Prince of Opera" and "melancholy."

A FOREIGN COURT

115 Heroics are but bravery to excess *1800*
   And genius is a state above the norm.
   When both combine how should a man express
   Those truths in dress? Sartorially conform?

   Or swagger to impress himself and those
   He leads in war when courage is a pose
   He must assume and trust his glory throws
   A blinding light upon his frightened foes?

   As will-power is refuelled by self-esteem
   And courage is the power of will applied
   A stimulant of swank and brag may seem
   Desirable when fear must be denied.

   So brightly shone his glamour as the gleam
   Of honours on his breast portrayed his dream.

116 When travelling home Vienna saw him chained
   By Emma's side "most like a dancing bear."
   Of public courtship moralists complained –
   The opera audience rose and cheered the pair.

   For when moralities are self imposed
   And regulate the conduct of a man
   Should human guidelines too long be opposed
   To natural forces god and devil can

   Become irrelevant, be swept aside
   By creativity, which some call lust
   And others love but which if long denied
   Ensures for each a progeny of dust.

   Prague, Dresden, Hamburg, down calm Elbe by sail –
   The Yarmouth packet laboured through a gale.

THE NORTHERN THREAT

1800-01

THE NORTHERN THREAT

117 Robed mayors, the crowds hurrahs and blaring bands   *1800*
With escorts of the mounted volunteers
And carriages man hauled by many hands
Amid the laughter and the happy tears

Of joyful welcome led the threesome on
Through Colchester and Ipswich to acclaim
In London for the hero. Not foregone
Was gossip on La Hamilton whose frame

Had undergone "extension" said the press,
"The Morning Herald", while "The Morning Post"
Declared her "swoln" augmenting the distress
Of Frances Nelson when it used the most

Explicit phrase on Emma's embonpoint,
One woman blooming and one woman wan.

118 Sir William Hamilton but not his wife,
To Nelson's chagrin, was required at Court
To meet a King whose offsprings' married life
Was lecherously untidy but that thought

Left George untroubled and he took the line
Convention must be heeded. Nelson went
With Hamilton, his uniform ashine
With foreign stars and orders. No consent

To wearing them had issued from the King
Who glanced and asked "I trust your health is good?"
Then turned his back too quick for answering
And with a General, as Nelson stood

In silent fury, talked at length of naught;
Correct behaviour by a snubbing taught.

THE NORTHERN THREAT

119   Applauded by the crowds yet made aware   *1800*
         Of disapproval by established powers,
         Stressed by his service, the incipient care
         Of furtive parenthood, by bitter hours

   In Fanny's presence Nelson showed his pique
   At dinner at the First Lord's when she peeled
   A wine glass full of walnuts but her meek
   And hopeful offering of help revealed

   The anger of a maimed and thwarted spouse
   Who with a sweeping gesture smashed the glass.
   In tears she left the table and the house.
   His rage and black frustration did not pass

   Before that wintery dawn when he'd decamped
   And nightlong through the streets of London tramped.

120   The Hamiltons and Nelsons at a play
         Drew audiences if management announced
         A box was booked and gave new lines to say
         To actors who proclaimed the French were trounced

   Or sang a Dibden patriotic song.
   At Drury Lane "Elvira's" tragic speech
   To end an act was equalled by the long
   Despairing sound of Lady Nelson's screech.

   In turban, feathers and a purple dress
   She fell while Nelson sat unmoved like stone;
   His father and his lover eased distress
   Caused when she heard the heroine intone

   "Now meet thy final peril, fearless man,
   An injured woman's fury if thou can."

THE NORTHERN THREAT

121 Though social disapproval was made plain *1801*
The government and Admiralty were set
On matching men to duties to maintain
Efficient fleets. The New Year's Day Gazette

Announced a new Vice Admiral of the Blue,
Lord Nelson, posted to the Channel Fleet
To board once more the "San Josef" which flew
The British colours following his feat

In capturing two Spanish men of war
Off Cape St Vincent under Jervis when
They read each other's minds four years before
And now were linked in comradeship again.

The day he left for Plymouth and Tor Bay
His wife left home and went her lonely way.

122 Emotions, bubbling like a choppy sea
When wind and tide cross on a harbour bar,
Beset and troubled him. A generous fee
Was paid at once to Frances and a far

More generous annuity arranged.
Their letters showed affection and respect –
Hers, wish to please; his, kindness though estranged.
Remembrance, conscience, duty stopped neglect.

Duty, the mark by which he always steered,
Delayed his coach at Honiton to call
Upon a widowed mother who appeared
Bereft by Westcott of "Majestic's" fall

But comforted by Admiral Nelson's smile
And gift of his own Medal of the Nile.

THE NORTHERN THREAT

123   "Poor man!" St Vincent wrote "he is devoured   *1801*
With vanity and folly" and was "strung
With ribbons and with medals" which were showered
By grateful courts upon him. Yet when hung

With ornaments he said he wished to miss
The ceremonies met with on his road.
St Vincent from Torre Abbey wrote that this
Was mere "pretence" while sorry "weakness" showed

In his infatuation. Emma's time
Was near and guiltily they used a code
When writing letters. Hidden like a crime
Horatia's birth meant joy must now implode

Within her father's heart. He was distressed
That happiness, like fears, should be suppressed.

124   Through lack of frigates Britain kept no grip
On Egypt's coast. In secret Buonaparte
Abandoned Kleber and embarked. His ship
With half his staff slunk homeward to the start

Of his dictatorship. This swift retreat,
Presented as a conqueror's return,
Although in fact strategical defeat,
Brought hero worshippers who had to learn

In years to come the bloody price of fame.
From Rhone to Seine he now need but appear,
Hear gravely every notable, a game
Continued when he tweaked some youngster's ear

And to that moonface, shining as its star,
Made flattering reference to their future gloire.

THE NORTHERN THREAT

125 In egocentric fury seeking power *1801*
Through flattering politics or coup d'etat
As Sieyes "sword" Napoleon matched the hour
When Directoire gave way to Consulat.

Three Consuls led, of whom he was the chief,
A France which sought to hold its spoils of war
The Rhine's left bank, the Scheldt, but his belief
Was also that the nation needed more

Efficiency at home, a breathing space
To mend each bridge, repair each rutted road
And build more ships before it could outface
The British fleets which off each French port rode

Incessantly in pitiless blockade
And halted much of Europe's sea-borne trade.

126 The British stopped and searched each neutral sail
For warlike goods or cargoes bound for France
Though sending manufactured goods for sale
To Turkey, Greece, to Portugal, the Hanse

To Russia and each Scandinavian port.
And while French merchant vessels sails were furled
In consequence of naval battles fought
The British traded freely round the world

And thereby nourished economic strengths
The means with which they bought such naval stores
As pitch and ropes and Baltic pine in lengths
To serve as masts and yards in current wars.

Yet irked by Britain's maritime control
The Baltic states essayed another role.

THE NORTHERN THREAT

127 With promptings from a jealous Russian Czar,   *1801*
Who wanted Malta as his satellite,
The Armed Neutrality was formed to bar
The British search of merchant ships, a rite

Disliked by Russians, Prussians, Danes and Swedes
Whom Buonaparte supported with his hosts
In Germany to block all British needs
For grain and masts and spars from Baltic coasts.

And Buonaparte believed a Baltic fleet
From those four powers combined could lure his foe
To serious damage eastward or defeat
And leave the Channel open for his blow.

An analytic Admiralty, adroit and cool,
Resolved to send the Corsican to school.

128 The hard St Vincent with his jutting chin
Which could be widened to an impish grin,
When justified, imposed fierce discipline
Upon his Channel captains and impelled them in

To closer watch upon each naval base.
In Yarmouth Roads a second fleet was formed
As Admiralty gave Nelson three days grace,
For private matters, when his heart was warmed

At first sight of Horatia, the child
He long had longed for and now briefly saw,
Then passed on from her nursery to the wild
March seas off Norfolk and a northern war

In which again he was subordinate;
His chief, though brave and senior, second rate.

THE NORTHERN THREAT

129 Hyde Parker was at sixty two a smart, *1801*
Small, dapper Admiral, a lady's man,
A widower who lost his hand and heart,
Re-wedding when the century began.

The Lady to this Knight was just sixteen
And for her husband organised a ball
Of which, of course, she would have been the queen.
As rockets rise, then so their sticks must fall

And Nelson, through St Vincent, stopped her flight
By writing to him, now the new First Lord,
Who hurried Parker's fleet off to its fight –
Time lost the loss that they could least afford.

Though not averse to dalliance or dance
Nelson gave precedence to thwarting France.

130 His flag flew in the shallow draught "St George",
A hook above the Dogger trawled for fish,
A turbot which it landed sent to forge
A link with Parker, a propitiatory dish

To satisfy that Admiral's known taste.
In bitter cold, with coughing crews the fleet
Hove to when in the Kattegat, a waste,
So Nelson thought, of time used up to meet

The Danish government. In Parker's view,
And as his orders read, the only way
To gain the Danes' consent to trade was through
Negotiations first. Then force. Delay

By "pen and ink men" made him chafe;
Said Nelson, "Boldest measures are most safe."

THE NORTHERN THREAT

131 The Foreign Office man who went ashore *1801*
Returned in dudgeon with the grave report
That British entry to the Sound meant war
While Danes were arming every hulk and fort.

To break their power Parker gave much thought
To waiting for the Balts to put to sea
And beating their united fleets. "You ought
To strike at once for we shall never be

As strong as now. Their strength can only grow."
Said Nelson who believed one beaten foe
Would mean the conflict's end. He urged a blow
At Copenhagen instantly. The slow

Deliberations of Hyde Parker met
A mind much quicker and a will more set.

132 Thus were the fears of fog and ice, the maze
Of possibilities, conflicting ways
Of solving all dilemmas and the haze
Of indecision melted by the blaze

Of Nelson's orb. To block the Swedish threat
Combined with Russian vessels not ice bound
Hyde Parker chose to split his fleet and set
His vessels out of forts' range in the Sound.

To overcome the Danes was Nelson's task.
He chose to loop the Middle Ground and steer
A northward course, surprisingly, and ask
For frigates and ten major ships to clear

The anchored gunline. Parker, unasked, gave
Two extra vessels, which was wise and brave.

THE NORTHERN THREAT

133 The zeal which Nelson carelessly displayed *1801*
Four years before at Santa Cruz remained
But lack of reconnoitring there betrayed
Himself and others. Now he was restrained

Before the Danish capital and spent
Two nights in taking soundings from a boat
In freezing fog between the banks and sent
Hardy by night to check which ships could float

Between the gun lined shore and Middle Ground.
Unlike the Nile his enemies were moored
Close in by bow and stern; thus to surround
Successive ships impossible. To board

And storm too costly, awkward facts which made
His only hope a furious cannonade.

134 Hyde Parker placed his bigger ships to check *2 Apr 1801*
An intervention from the north or east
As Nelson's pilots, much in fear of wreck
Nosed round the Middle Ground; a fear at least

Well justified when "Agamemnon" struck,
"Bellona" followed shortly and the bank
Detained a third ship when the "Edgar" stuck.
The fault, said Nelson, was his own. A frank

Assessment later owned that last survey,
Which Hardy made in silence with a pole
To hush the splash of lead, outlined the way
To victory. He cursed the pilots' role

Who thought "their silly heads were clear of shot."
Yet grounded where the Danish fire was hot.

THE NORTHERN THREAT

135   The onset of the stately British van   *2 Apr 1801*
Dispersed by tide on shoals in disarray
Removed those ships which Nelson's detailed plan
Laid down would bring their heavy guns to play

Upon the Three Crowns Battery which barred
The Copenhagen harbour mouth and raked
The passage to that port. Thus Riou, ill starred,
In "Amazon" five frigates led and staked

His own and small crews' lives to mask the blast
Of those Trekroner guns which could be laid
To fire upon the British ships which cast
Their anchors by the Danes to cannonade.

"Formidable to those who know not war."
Said Nelson of the hulks beside the shore.

136   The rapid movement of his 'fin' was stopped,
Pre-action agitation disappeared,
The instant Danish cannon balls were dropped
About his flagship "Elephant" which steered

Against the puthering gunports of the Danes
And broadside after shattering broadside poured
Through oaken bulwark and pine deck where stains
Of blood spread wider as the cannon roared

And Nelson's tetchy nervousness gave way
To calm and smiles when splinters from a mast
Spiked round about. A soldier heard him say
With twinkling eye. "Warm work. It cannot last."

He checked his walk "Mark you I would not be
"Elsewhere for thousands!" he proclaimed with glee.

THE NORTHERN THREAT

137   His orb shone then and pacified such fears   *2 Apr 1801*
As inwardly he felt. All play a game
Who are as heroes ranked when danger nears
And mock the horrors, possibly for fame

Or else, light-heartedly, to re-assure
Themselves and others that the flea-bite death
Is of no consequence or has allure
If the pursuit of 'honour' stops the breath.

So now, beset by thunder, Nelson paced
His width of deck wreathed in the cannon smoke
And through the chaos and inferno traced
Irregularities of sound which spoke

Of faltering gunfire by the Danes, now doomed
As metronomic British broadsides boomed.

138   Up-wind off-shore Hyde Parker scanned the stage
Whereon this bloody tragedy was played
In which his heavy ships could not engage
Because they swam too deeply. Unallayed

By his Flag Captain's view that they must wait
Frustration fed his fears. The "London" flew
The signal to break off the fight but great
Was Nelson's fury. "Damn me if I do."

He ordered that "Close Action" should remain
His masthead flag with which all must comply.
"I have a right to blindness." With disdain
He raised his spy glass to his blind right eye

"I do not see the signal" was the claim
Which clinched this playwright-actor-hero's fame.

THE NORTHERN THREAT

139 The recall signal was perceived by Riou – *2 Apr 1801*
Smoke hid the masthead flag which Nelson flew –
He followed orders; "Amazon" withdrew
And he by raking fire was cut in two.

And almost as those fatal shots were fired
"Oh, what will Nelson think of us?" Riou cried;
He knew the craven and the weak retired
To greater danger but obeyed and died.

And simultaneously the Danish force
Lost drifting hulks while "Dannebrog" was caught
By blazing fires, the south wind set her course
As "Elephant" with "Elefanten" fought.

To end the senseless killing Nelson wrote
Upon the tiller head an urgent note.

140 To "England's brothers" Nelson now appealed
To stop the fight. He called for wax to seal
The note. A wafer's covering revealed
Disquiet and haste he said. The Danes would feel

He stood in need of peace. A cannon ball
Took off the seaman's head who went to bring
A candle and the wax. A second call
Let Nelson seal the missive with his ring.

And Captain Thesiger was rowed ashore
Beneath a flag of truce and found the Prince
Beside the sally port. A Prince who bore
No animus for England. To convince

Himself of her intentions he enquired
Her reasons and the terms which were desired.

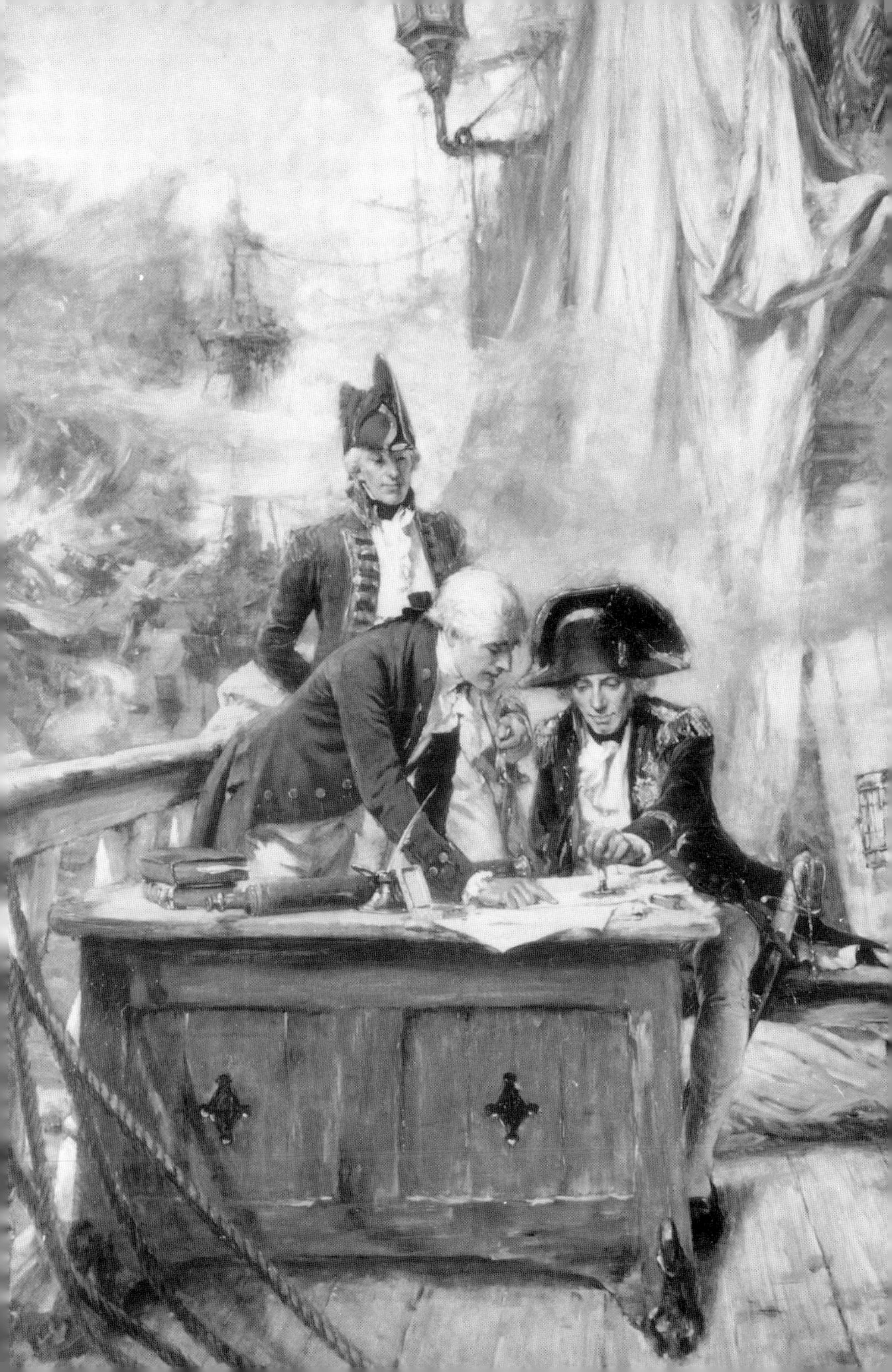

THE NORTHERN THREAT

141 A truce allowed the Danes to take ashore *2 Apr 1801*
Their many casualties for when men fell
Surviving officers called forward more
Trained gunners. Student volunteers as well

Were rushed aboard each riddled wooden hull
Which double banked the wounded and the dead,
While British ships had surgeons' cockpits full
And scuppers on the "Monarch" dribbled red.

She lost ten score and ten, the greatest loss
A British warship suffered in that war
With France and her supporters, while across
The gunline Danish dead on ship or shore

Exceeded Britain's. Danes endured four hours;
Nelson thought one enough for other powers.

142 "Humanity" claimed Nelson was the cause
For which he sought a truce. He held that Danes
And English were related and the pause
He called for must result in mutual gains.

Hyde Parker sent him to negotiate
The cease fire through a sullen Danish crowd
Whose Prince made little effort to debate
The easy terms his enemy allowed.

Removal of the prizes; British right
To trade into the Baltic; three month's ban
On Danish ships re-armament; the fight
Achieved all Britain's aims when she began

Unnecessary action which was fought
When regicide had changed the Russian court.

THE NORTHERN THREAT

143   The news of an assassinated Czar   *1801*
Reached Copenhagen when the fight was done.
Ironically the dead man sought to bar
All British trade but his reformist son

Was prompt to change that policy which made
A Baltic conflict futile. Nelson fought
Not knowing drunken officers had played
Their stranglers' role in Petersburgh and brought

Czar Alexander in to follow Paul
Eight days before a thousand patriots died
Who if Hyde Parker's wife had held her ball
Need not have perished for their nation's pride.

The urgent zest of Nelson killed them all –
And also brought Hyde Parker's prompt recall.

144   With hindsight ironies can be descried.
Contemporaries simply saw the need
To master England's foes or to divide
One from another and to praise the deed

When this was done. In victory's aftermath
Nelson complained of illness and desired
To leave the fleet although he paced the path
Of duty when St Vincent still required

His presence in the Baltic in command.
His chests were lifted from the home bound ship
Which carried Parker to a life on land
And instantly the fleet felt Nelson's grip.

"Weigh anchor" was his first command. Intense
And instant action was to him good sense.

THE NORTHERN THREAT

145 To Revel and the Russians was the course *1801*
Which Nelson set and there learned their intent
To free all British merchant ships. His force,
Not needed even as a threat, was sent

Again towards Sweden and the Kattegat
First having charted harbour mouths and forts
In Revel and Karlscrona, noting that
The wooden quays would blaze in both those ports

If men o' war took refuge from attack.
Nelson declared the Baltic fleets at sea
Could easily be beaten through their lack
Of joint manoeuvre practice, mastery

In naval war requiring an entire
Fleet concentrate great weight and rate of fire.

146 The campaign over and its aim achieved
An argument about awards began
As Nelson, sickly, begged to be relieved
The rumour ran the government did not plan

To issue medals for the Danes' defeat
Despite the precedents of Camperdown,
St Vincent and the Nile. The Baltic Fleet
Had taken prizes but a stingy Crown

Refused to pay for captured vessels sunk
On Parker's orders while he feared the Swedes
And Russians might attack. Some spoke of funk
While hyperbolic Nelson feared his deeds

Led to "a debtors' prison" if his fame
Did not add extra pennies to his name.

THE NORTHERN THREAT

147 The "London" and "St George" were of a size *1801*
Unseen upon the southern Baltic coast
And drew big crowds which also knew the ties
Of Mecklenburgh to England. As the host

Aboard his flagship Nelson found the Duke
Brought out a hundred other guests to see
His sister's husband's fleet. He felt rebuke
From Court would follow if he seemed to be

Restrained in welcoming a lumpish guest
Of sixty one who pleasured in the thumps
Of gun salutes. His ladies at their best
Were plain and sturdy but at worst were frumps.

In London Nelson's raising was announced
To Viscount for another nation trounced.

148 Admirers thought this honour was too low
And should have been awarded for the Nile
As Viscounts are, like Barons, ranked below
Earls, Marquesses and Dukes. Yet higher style

Was not judged fitting as detached command
Placed ultimate responsibility
On others who, at least in theory, planned
Successful actions. The ability

Of chief commanders who were not engaged
To claim far more prize cash than those who fought
Was naval custom but it so enraged
A hard up Nelson that he took to court

His friend St Vincent, whom he much admired,
And fought an action neither man desired.

THE NORTHERN THREAT

149   At 4 a.m. each morning Foley sent   1801
      Warm milk to Nelson stricken by both 'flu
      And chest complaints. His thoughts were bent
      On death afloat but knew an anxious crew

      Cared greatly for him and his letters show
      Self-pity modified by open pride
      In their affection. Though he stayed below
      For twenty days strict discipline applied

      To all fleet business and he recognised
      A Rostock cartel doubling the rate
      For bread, flour, cheese and beef, so organised
      Supplies from Dantzic at a large rebate.

      He eaked out Britain's gold; his close control
      Of quality of food a greater role.

150   Relief by Admiral Pole. A brig, the "Kite",
      Bounced Nelson back to England. He was sick,
      As always in small ships, and wrote this plight
      Was quite incurable. He made a quick

      Tour round the Yarmouth hospital to see
      The Copenhagen wounded. From a maimed
      But active Admiral that proved to be
      A gesture welcomed by the blind, the lamed

      And crippled victims of a foolish war
      Who like their countrymen both rich and poor
      United in their national pride and saw
      This battered man, who put their weal before

      His own, a hero for whom all should sing
      "God save Lord Nelson!" and "God Save The King."

THE LONG CHASE

1801–05

THE LONG CHASE

151   Though thwarted in the Baltic Buonaparte   *1801*
        Amassed an army on the north French coast
        And planned that troop filled open boats should start
        Invasion when the coast was clear. His boast

        That veteran French would quickly overcome,
        When once ashore, the British volunteers
        Roused anger, hate and ribaldry but some
        Old women of both sexes voiced their fears

        Of rapine, pillage and the fleet's defeat.
        The Admiralty to lighten this distress
        Appointed Nelson to the inshore fleet
        Which ranged from Beachy Head to Orfordness.

        "The French *may* come." St Vincent said with glee
        "I only say they cannot come by sea."

152   The citizens of Dover lined their cliff
        To hear Lord Nelson "speaking to the French."
        A cannonade which taught Boulogne a stiff
        And bloody lesson. Barricade and trench

        And upper town were spared but bomb and ball
        Were poured upon the harbour and the mole
        From frigates, mortar ships and small
        But handy English vessels. This the role

        Of "Cracker", "Boxer", "Bruiser", "Haughty", "Fame",
        "Attacker" and "Defender". Each became
        A "Brave" "Upholder" of its "Valiant" name
        While 'carcasses', the mortar boats, spread flame

        By lobbing bombs on craft massed by the quay
        As inshore squadron vessels cleared the sea.

THE LONG CHASE

153   Reports from shipyards and each waterway   1801
      In Zealand or beside the Scheldt agreed
      The boat construction programme under way
      Was Buonaparte's, surpassing local need.

      And Nelson noted Flushing as the key
      To lock this door. Invaders could not row
      To England thence. Yet, if they sailed to sea
      Cross tides, banks, currents with a helpful blow

      From south or east, he thought no cockleshell
      Would voyage further than three miles from land
      Before his ravening ships spewed out their hell
      And strewed the wrecks and corpses on the sand.

      To animate his men he left the Nore
      To speak to all who served on ship or shore.

154   He asked if government was prepared to fight
      Ashore at Flushing with 5,000 men
      But, while they pondered, planned a raid at night
      With 20 boat crews on Boulogne again.

      He aimed to capture gunboats, tow them out
      And show the French invasion had to fail
      Which, by a paradox, he proved about
      Expected landings. He could not prevail

      As boats delayed by wind and tide missed cues,
      Attacked in piece meal fashion craft chained fast
      To land or neighbours and with well armed crews
      Behind a frieze of iron spikes. The blast

      Of musket vollies piled the English dead
      On English wounded as the sea ran red.

THE LONG CHASE

155   In Deal where Nelson sat beside his bed   1801
        His aide young Edward Parker's shattered thigh
        Was taken off. He rallied but was dead
        Within the month and Nelson's strangled cry

        "He was my child. I found him in distress."
        Displayed frustrated fatherhood, the toll
        Of deep emotion longing to express
        Itself in creativity, a role

        The coldness of his wife denied. A house,
        Romanticised in letters as "the farm"
        Was bought unseen by him. His real spouse,
        His Emma, acting as his lost right arm,

        Bought Merton with his money in his name
        Where she, together with Sir William, came.

156   The war with Buonaparte now petered out   1802
        Resulting in "experimental peace"
        An armistice, a stalemate brought about
        By joint exhaustion and foreseen increase

        In British trade, a hope long unfulfilled
        Through vetos by Napoleon who proclaimed
        Himself as Emperor and henceforward willed
        He and his dynasty would be so named.

        In March the Peace of Amiens was signed
        And France regained most territories lost
        To British sea power. Nelson, who resigned
        His coastal post, won liberty. The cost

        Half pay at home. His peace of mind and health
        And happy home he valued more than wealth.

THE LONG CHASE

157   The British government hoped for prosperous peace.   *1802*
Napoleon looked to war to fuel his pride
Sea lanes were freed yet slaughter did not cease
Like Brest's blockade, for 20,000 died

From war and yellow fever when he sent
An expedition thence to overcome
Revolted Haitian slaves. That would have spent
French blood to earn cheap sugar cane or rum

Yet garnered odium as the French reward
With liberty despited, brotherhood
Abandoned and equality ignored.
His western dream, Napoleon understood,

Was pointless once America saw plain
The threat implied by France allied to Spain.

158   In France the trade with colonies was seen
As worth more than industrial success
Yet Creole influence from Josephine
Plus planters' pleas and mercantile distress

Weighed less than strategy. Napoleon saw
Persistence in the western hemisphere
Could link the States to Britain in a war
Through which French naval vessels could not steer.

Thus Jefferson, who guessed Napoleon planned
To rule all Europe, and the east, with west
A Franco-Spanish Empire overland
Atlantic to Pacific, thought it best

Monroe should shop in Paris, from which dates
Louisiana's purchase by the States.

THE LONG CHASE

159 Through Midland England on a six weeks tour *1802/:*
   To Wales the Hamiltons gave happiness
   To Nelson, as at Merton. But the poor
   Fond parents of Horatia more or less

   Hid truth with fictions of a widow's child
   Supported out of charity. In play
   Upon the floor the father was beguiled
   And joyfully enslaved; then called away

   Once more to London by the First Sea Lord
   Who said command off Toulon was his due
   If war broke out again. A strong accord
   With William Hamilton remained all through

   That life and on his deathbed Emma fanned
   And clasped his head while Nelson held his hand.

160 In Nelson's house at Merton Emma made
   A haven for him which some criticised
   As flattering her hero. It displayed
   So many relics as to be despised

   As "tasteless" one censorious critic claimed.
   Yet Nelson there was happy to be lapped
   In his achievements. Hoppner shows him maimed,
   Star studded coat, by sashes tightly wrapped,

   A central parting to the greying hair
   Divided like a bow wave either side,
   Full mouth, resolved, with compressed lips, a stare
   Direct, commanding yet the eyes, set wide,

   Show wisdom and compassion. Stern, serene
   He broods before a background battle scene.

THE LONG CHASE

161   Intelligence reports which were received   *1803*
In London showed Napoleon plotted still
To send an army eastward. Undeceived
The British government resolved until

This threat to India was removed they must
Be placed to have such French manoeuvres watched
By line o' battle ships so that a thrust
If made towards Egypt could be quickly scotched.

That policy required a naval base.
With Malta held conveniently at hand
The British now refused to cede the place
Despite Napoleon's furious demand.

He ranted at a calm ambassador
His two hour tirade threatening endless war.

162   Frustration fired the anger of a man
Intent on domination who had been
Coralled in little Europe by the span
Of sea power setting limits to his scene

Of action and the stage on which he played.
Administrative genius underpinned
Improvements in French life. Had he delayed
Renewal of his quarrel then the wind

Of change within his nation might have turned
The weather vane of fortune and the star
He said he followed far more brightly burned
Than Nelson's golden orb which glowed afar.

Romantic dreamers both, these men of war
Yet one indifferent to the moral law.

THE LONG CHASE

163	The amoral Napoleon commenced	*180*
	To reinforce his navy with a spate
	Of ships built in the south and west. He sensed
	His foe was time and speeded up the rate

	Of dockyard work. Tired oxen on the long
	And rutted roads of France hauled to the coast
	On timber drags the trunks to form the strong
	Ships' frameworks or bring Baltic stores when most

	French cabotage induced an English raid.
	Artillery on headlands helped boats creep
	From bay to bay, protecting trickle trade
	While ingenuity let shipwrights reap

	The profit in the dockyard of Rochefort
	From harnessing a windmill to a saw.

164	The energy with which the French pursued
	Their building programme brought a launching rate
	Of one large ship a fortnight and renewed
	Napoleon's hope his navy could equate

	In size to Britain's and let him invade
	Across the Channel but this view ignored
	The fact that when new battleships were made
	They had no power without trained crews aboard.

	And France had fewer merchant ships from which
	To levy seamen while her fishing fleet
	Was smaller than the British. Knot and hitch
	Or clew or furl or block or shroud or sheet

	Were strange to crews Napoleon called on then;
	He had the better ships; not better men.

THE LONG CHASE

165   Despite reforms so vigorously urged   *1803*
France suffered now for every past mistake;
When loyal royalist officers were purged
Or Huguenots were massacred to break

The Protestants who served a Catholic king,
As, in the Terror, Catholics were forced
To be apostates or enjoy the sting
Of Madame Guillotine who soon divorced

Four hundred heads from necks in Rennes and Brest.
In Finisterre, Charente and La Vendee
The Chouans' struggle in the wasted West
Wiped out whole coastal villages which may

Have manned Napoleon's ships had civil war
Not slaughtered all a dozen years before.

166   The Swiss were conquered and Piedmont annexed;
Aggression Britain deemed the final straw,
So, neither fearful nor perplexed but vexed,
She sailed her squadrons, thus renewing war

For twelve years on the Continent and changed
The history of the World. A close blockade
Of bases was begun again which ranged
Around all Western Europe and displayed

From Toulon to the Texel that a chain
Of warships was as flexible and strong
As leg irons used to fetter or restrain
A criminal, or Emperor, in the wrong.

In "Victory" from Portsmouth Nelson sailed:
French Toulon ships were virtually jailed.

"Victory" off Spithead   James Brereton

THE LONG CHASE

167 To lure them to escape then face a fight *1803–4*
Was Nelson's aim. His frigates near the coast
Were bait and look-outs. He kept out of sight
Of Toulon whose commander made the boast

That at Boulogne he beat off every boat
And now made Nelson once again retire.
"He'll eat his words. I'll stuff them down his throat."
The prowling cat said of this mousehole liar.

But Nelson, as allusive letters show,
Was privately near frantic for the health
Of Emma who was soon to undergo,
Confinement once again in furtive stealth.

Miscarriage, still birth, or an infant death?
No record even shows the child drew breath.

168 The British kept the sea the winter through
Despite their "crazy" ships need for repairs,
And benefited from attention to
The diet of crews, the chief of Nelson's cares.

He used his multilingual chaplain Scott
For vegetable buying and for meat
Brought fresh from nearby ports to stop the rot
That scurvy and salt pork could give a fleet.

And oranges and wine in lieu of rum
Or beer that soured and scoured, plus lemons' juice
Offset ship's biscuit that as well as crumb
When tapped shed weevil. Wise and generous use

Of government funds thus saved the nation's wealth;
"No sick" he wrote. "All crews in robust health."

THE LONG CHASE

169 He cared for government's pennies and ordained *1804*
Three captains should most carefully enquire
About wet flour; then forcibly complained
That issue Guernsey 'frocks' rucked inches higher

Than waistbands when men worked upon the yards.
A greater length the Admiralty was told
Was needed or bad chills were on the cards.
He grumbled in his letters of the cold,

Of being "almost blind", of "being fagged",
Of "being sea-sick, always tossed about"
Of other Admirals' wealth. His spirit sagged
In private though his kindness bubbled out

At Merton when a ticking watch appeared
With gloves made from Sardinian mussel beard.

170 La Touche Treville, commanding in Toulon,
Died from a heart attack. The French believed
That frequent climbs to look-out posts brought on
His death. Sardonic Nelson was not grieved

That search for British ships had this effect;
"I always said that that would be his end."
Napoleon, to remedy defect,
Thought Villeneuve "lucky" and the man to send

To outwit Nelson. If he passed that test
His squadron with the rest must concentrate
So Villeneuve had, to link Toulon with Brest,
Iberia to circumnavigate,

Then whether wind blew east, north, west or south,
He needed victory in the Channel's mouth.

THE LONG CHASE

171   Napoleon's plan to concentrate his fleet   *1805*
With Spain's envisaged squadrons sailing west
To junction in the Antilles, a feat
Preceding rapid rendezvous off Brest.

This perfect paper exercise ignored
Ship handling, elements of chance, of war
Of storm, of disrepair, of sick aboard
Or fleet commanders with a moral flaw.

The moral factor, so Napoleon said,
Outweighs material means by three to one,
A truth enlarged, yet once Villeneuve had fled
From Aboukir his self belief was gone.

While Nelson held one breeze harmed more French sails
Than his fleet suffered from all winter's gales.

172   For two and twenty months the British sailed
About the "Gulf of Lions" without a spar
Lost overboard. Although French vessels failed
To stay at sea in half a gale when far

From enemies they finally put out
Upon Napoleon's orders from Toulon
To hurry west at night and left a doubt
In Nelson's mind about which way they'd gone.

He steered at first to parry any blow
At Naples, Egypt or the Turkish Porte
Then piled his canvas on to chase the slow
Villeneuve who left, unwilling to be caught

Off Murcia, Spanish allies shipping stores
And so broke out to fight Atlantic wars.

THE LONG CHASE

173   What of the man by whom he was pursued   *1805*
Three thousand miles each way from shore to shore?
A patriot by duty bound. Imbued
With faith. Implacable. Three years before

His mien was caught by Hoppner; lengthy lips
Determined, solemn, sensual; yet one eye
Which sparkles near to laughter; distant ships
Close locked in war and black cloud drifting by

Above the dull eye and the empty sleeve.
A face disdaining death, a mind which thought
That through the body's loss he could retrieve
Great profit from the glory which he sought.

Beyond Gibraltar empty ocean spread
And nothing showed where Villeneuve had fled.

174   The expertise which British Admirals brought
To naval matters stretched beyond the dull
Minutiae of sea skills. War had taught
The need for thinking globally. A full

Acquaintance with realities of power
Informed their thought and made initiative
A constant need. Off Cadiz in an hour
Sir John Orde turned his squadron north to give

Support off Brest to Gardner and secure
The Channel's mouth as Villeneuve passed the Rock
While Nelson read Orde's mind and sensed French lure
For Caribbean conquests. He took stock

When watering ships at Lagos where his views
Were firmed when Admiral Campbell brought him news.

THE LONG CHASE

175   Campbell, a Scot, long served the Portuguese,   *1805*
      Blockading Malta after Aboukir.
      His masters now were neutral but to ease
      His British conscience, ending his career,

      He boarded "Victory" and conveyed his thoughts.
      Villeneuve, he said, with Spanish ships combined
      Had sailed from Cadiz for West Indian ports,
      Which matched the picture Nelson had in mind.

      He feared Jamaica was the likely prize
      For French troops carried in the men o' war
      So set sails instantly. He read the skies
      For signs of wind yet pressing west foresaw

      Wrong destination guessing damn his name
      Or late arrival carry equal blame.

176   He could have headed north to bolt the door
      Cornwallis held across the Channel's mouth,
      A greater concentration to ensure
      Great Britain's safety but he headed south

      And west in late pursuit, a month behind.
      His ten ships of the line made gains each day
      Upon a gaggle of eighteen combined
      With six big frigates, shortening their stay

      In Caribbean waters. Villeneuve watched
      All through an August night the blinding light
      Of Aboukir, a memory which scotched
      His innate courage and induced his flight

      Again towards France when presently he learned
      His hunter had implacably returned.

THE LONG CHASE

177   Inaccurate reports about his foes   1805
      Who threaded through the Leeward Islands' maze
      Diverted Nelson as he sought to close
      With Villeneuve. He analysed the ways

      The Frenchman's mind worked. Empathy allied
      To guestimates of how French orders ran
      His only tools – which leaders though supplied
      With radio, satellite and radar scan

      Must still employ. Montgomery's caravan
      Held more than maps, for Rommel's photographs
      Adorned a wall, long gazed at so the man
      Was studied just as closely as the paths

      By jebels and through wadis on towards Rome.
      Said Nelson "Villeneuve will make for home."

178   The French fleet, sickly, left in Martinique
      Five hundred dead and put its troops ashore,
      A penny packet proving far too weak
      To offer fight when later in the war

      The British had command of all the seas.
      Five days behind her foe the "Victory" sailed
      Quite free of sickness, reaping every breeze
      With sickled canvas when the French had failed

      To damage fatally West Indian trade.
      The stately flagship dipping from each crest
      Outpaced the barnacled "Superb". Afraid
      Her Captain Keats would worry that his best

      Endeavours were derided Nelson wrote
      To him for all his crew a "Well Done" note.

THE LONG CHASE

179 Humanity, good manners, kindly ways 1805
Which balanced ruthless bravery in war
Won Nelson's seamen's hearts. He spent his days
In dignity with music played before

Main meals when crystal glass and porcelain
Improved appearance of the food and wine
While "Hearts of Oak's" inspiring strain
Preceded officers who went to dine

And savoured at that family parade
The bandsmen's audible aperitif,
Both national paean and a serenade,
Which praised Old England and her famed Roast Beef.

The Chaplain said his grace and rendered thanks –
At midnight Nelson noticed floating planks.

180 Three planks upon a calm and lonely sea
Lit by the moon or a phosphoric glow
Upon midsummer night brought "misery",
His quill recorded when he went below.

He thought they floated from the other fleet
And was "most miserable" but also wrote
That feeling was "most foolish". Incomplete
Intelligence meant blindness when afloat

Yet when from "Victory" Nelson stepped ashore,
Two years bar ten days constantly at sea,
Gibraltar's garrison knew nothing more
Than that the Straits from Villeneuve were free.

He hurried on, towards Ushant setting course;
Cornwallis cruised there with sufficient force.

THE LONG CHASE

181 Moreover Nelson heard the hoped for news *1805*
That Calder's squadron west of Finisterre
Had intercepted Villeneuve's autumn cruise
And though outnumbered made his ships repair

To Vigo, Ferrol and French western ports
While capturing two Spanish ships, a feat
Which failed to please the nation. British thoughts,
Like Nelson's, sought destruction of a fleet.

No partial victory now could calm the fear
Frustration, anger, threatened Britons felt
Although their hero Nelson made it clear
That with the way in war that cards are dealt

"I might have done like Calder – or less well.
The outcome of a battle none can tell."

182 Home came the hero, home from distant seas
Home to beloved Merton, cared for, kempt,
Where blessed Emma ever sought to please
Her Nelson who let love alone pre-empt

Pursuit of glory and who daily wrote
With love and admiration when apart
The passion pulsing through each hurried note,
His golden orb subservient to his heart.

Domestic dreams fulfilled. The household's head
At table sat with relatives and friends;
Talked with his gardener, planned a flower bed
Or sited saplings, sought for colour blends

And spoke of vistas or how sunlight fell
On his small landscape. Blackwood broke the spell.

THE LONG CHASE

183   Past noon one Sunday Nelson went to Pitt   *1805*
And told the Premier Villeneuve would take
His force to Toulon, thereby freeing it
From all blockades. His 70 ships would make

It "difficult" for Britain to prevail
Against the Spaniards and the French combined.
He thought this new Armada would set sail
For Britain, yet if Collingwood could find

A separated squadron or half fleet
Between Gibraltar and Cadiz all fear
Of Channel war would melt with its defeat.
Pitt nodded and immediately made clear

Nelson must take command if Villeneuve moved –
A posting which the Admiralty approved.

184   A frigate captain clattering up the drive
Of Merton found at daybreak Nelson dressed
As if expecting orders to arrive.
"You bring me news!" called Nelson then expressed

The view that "I shall have to beat them yet!"
When told in haste "My Lord, the Biscay fleet
From France and Spain is in Cadiz." They met
But briefly, Blackwood turning to complete

His post haste race from Portsmouth and from Spain
Went hammering up the dusty London road.
His Admiral followed, knowing war again
Would call him from his briefly known abode.

"No thought of self is possible" he sighed.
His loved but powerless Emma quietly cried.

THE LONG CHASE

185 The ante-room of Castlereagh became *1805*
By chance for near an hour the meeting place
Of Wellesley and Nelson, men whose fame
Endures to-day for deeds which changed the face

Of Europe and a wider world and stopped
A tyrant's bloody passage in its track.
The future Wellington said Nelson dropped
His bragging postures "when on coming back

From asking who I was" his manner changed
From being "vain and silly" and he talked
As "officers and statesmen" should and ranged
The world strategically in depth. Uncorked

Like quality champagne his thoughts fizzed out
"A most superior man without a doubt."

186 His Merton home was packed with relatives
That evening when he finally returned
From Admlralty. A great commander lives
His private life in public which he learned

From shipboard pressures that restrict a man
To taking pleasure from the public good,
Though privately, as Nelson did, he can
"Pursue his orb", which shipmates understood,

More simply, as devoted duty done.
Respectful crowds pressed round him in the street
And when at home he could not be alone
For, knowing he must leave to lead the fleet,

Guests daily called at Merton, dined and slept.
That night "when all at table" Emma wept.

THE LONG CHASE

187 In prayer beside his daughter's bed he knelt *1805*
Then "left at dear, dear Merton all I hold
As dear in this world." Strong emotions felt
At midnight, when his horses changed, unfold

In scratchy diary entries which he wrote
Lamplit in Guildford as he went "to serve
My king and country." And with lump in throat
Implored his God to grant he might deserve

Fulfilment of his country's hopes yet still
Return to praise the God whom he adored.
But should it be "good Providence's will"
To "cut" his days on earth, then in accord

"I bow with great submission." He relied
On God to care for Emma if he died.

188 He breakfasted in Portsmouth. From "The George"
Beset by crowds he walked to Southsea beach
Regretting that he lacked one hand to forge
More links with friends. His smiles and gentle speech

Enraptured all. Some knelt, some cheered, some cried.
As Nelson's name was blessed by every lip,
Escorting troops were brusquely pushed aside,
And citizens convoyed him towards his ship.

His bargemen pulled for "Victory" as he raised
His hat to knee-deep watchers by the shore
And said he had their hearts now, God be praised,
Whereas he only had their cheers before.

To end his five and twenty days ashore
Broad "Victory" beat down Channel seeking war.

Nelson embarking from Southsea

TRAFALGAR

1805

TRAFALGAR

189 Beyond four days' horizons pitched the fleet *1805*
In patience but impatient for the hour
When Nelson joined. All dreamed of the defeat
Of French and Spaniards. "Oh, ye men of power

Send us Lord Nelson" one Commander wrote
When bored by Collingwood's most strict blockade
Of Cadiz where a forest seemed afloat,
Ranked allied masts, unsteady on parade,

Which bobbed or rocked and curtsied to the tide
Observed by British frigates on patrol
In swell or equinoctial gale outside
Safe Cadiz harbour's "spit of land" and mole

While distant line of battle squadrons rode
Land tethered by a silent signal code.

190 Howe and Home Popham grouping coloured flags
Which matched taut word and phrase lists got to grips
With age old signal problems, cutting lags
In message sending, so the talking ships,

Swift frigates spread to westward in a chain
Of links at limits of their yeomens' sight,
Sailed north to south and turning north again
Were Nelson's eyes before the coming fight.

He sent ahead to warn that no salute
That might betray his coming should be fired
For fear the French in fear of his repute
Would stay in port to foil what he desired –

Fleet action of a type he had designed
With Nelson sighted while Villeneuve was blind.

TRAFALGAR

191   His coming to the fleet caused "general joy"   *1805*
A zest and happiness he shared and spread
Not quite suppressing, like an eager boy,
Excitement when adventure lay ahead.

Yet overall the discipline and skill
Which seamen need to live upon the sea
Prevailed as did his inspirational will
Which gave his crews and ships their unity.

Now country shipping was allowed to sell
Fresh fruit once more to vessels in the fleet
And Nelson dined his captains well to tell
Them of his plans for utter French defeat.

Thus tedium turned to eagerness at drill
The way to safety being speed to kill.

192   The plan he now expounded was to sail
To windward and wear inward when the line
Of allied ships was formed and then assail
To plunge a Neptune's trident through its spine

By three divisions turning out of line –
Not wasting time to form for the attack –
Each thrusting with an Admiral at its tine
To pierce the foe and let the wind hold back

His van to leeward, exiled from the fight.
Then in the general melee Nelson said
Each British captain would be in the right
To lie beside an enemy. His dread

Was lack of time to conquer. Short daylight
In late October would curtail the fight.

TRAFALGAR

193 And Emma read, so proudly, of two nights *1805*
     When Admirals and Captains dined aboard
     In "Victory's" stateroom and the lantern lights
     Lit dark mahogany as wine was poured.

   While eager Nelson told them of his scheme
   To turn from line ahead and charge their foes
   All realised it would fulfil the dream
   Of forcing general action and impose

   The peace of conquest, ending national fear.
   "The 'Nelson Touch' moved some to tears" he wrote
   It struck them "like electric shock" to hear
   A plan so "new and simple." Thus their vote

   "From Admirals downwards" was that all desired
   To show "approval" and were "friends inspired".

194 Sir Robert Calder's fight off Finisterre
     When Spanish ships surrendered had been fought
     In desultory fashion without flair
     The Admiralty and Britain's public thought.

   No partial victories could satisfy
   An angry nation which recalled the Nile
   And Dutch and Danish victories to deny
   Napoleon ships. Thus Bobbie Calder's bile

   When thought a poltroon led to his demand
   For military trial to clear his name.
   The Admiralty agreed. "I understand
   A brother officer's dismay." That shame

   Led Nelson to despatch him on his trip
   In "Prince of Wales" his 98 gun ship.

TRAFALGAR

195   This gesture which deprived the fleet of force   *1805*
When frigate, brig or schooner would have served
Displayed emotion and that deep resource
Of kindness, more than Calder then deserved,

Which hallmarked Nelson as a man who cared
For all below him, confident his plan
Won hearts' approval for the things he dared.
Quixoticism in a lesser man.

Now outward show reflected inward grace
As ships unbidden copied "Victory's" bands
Of black on orange gun ports while a brace
Of rings round masts were painted so all hands,

Nelson ordaining that it should be so,
More readily could tell a friend from foe.

196   To tempt Villeneuve to venture out of port
The British line of battle shifted west
While Blackwood's rapid frigates kept a taut
Unblinking watch on Cadiz with that zest

And constant discipline imposed at sea
By wave and wind which night and day demand
Exact attention. The Pandora's key
To Villeneuve's chest of troubles was command

Of inexperienced and unpractised crews
Whose slow reactions must ensure defeat.
He sensed such failure yet upon the news
Of his successor coming bade his fleet

"Hoist sail" as Blackwood signalled that he thought
"The enemy is coming out of port."

TRAFALGAR

197 The French and Spaniards straggled out to sea *1805*
Aware a British squadron was detached
To water in Gibraltar. Louis' plea
To stay with Nelson when he was despatched

Just days before for victualling was refused.
The first to go would be the first returned
As all must go he should not feel misused
His hero told him knowing that he yearned

To finish work which when a 'Crocodile'
Eight years before together they began
With overwhelming victory at the Nile.
Yet Louis' absence now meant that the plan

To cleanse the waters with a trident must
Be altered to a two pronged pitch fork thrust.

198 And Villeneuve, that sad and harried man,
A Provencal who said he wished he were
Among his grey leaved olive trees, began
His last manoeuvres knowing he'd incur

His Emperor's anger if he failed to sail
And Spanish hindrance if he put to sea
With allies whose unhandy ships would fail
To keep their stations. He most probably

Sought death with honour as the way to solve
Insoluble dilemma. Nelson sought
His foe's destruction though that could involve
His own decease, a likelihood he thought

Addiction to his golden orb would bring
In service to his Country and his King.

TRAFALGAR

199   Throughout the dark of an October night   *20/21 Oct 1805*
In lurking "Euryalus" Blackwood saw
The looms on skyline or the glints of light
Where French and Spaniards wallowed out to war.

With gunshots on the hour or Bengal flare
He signalled Nelson with the course they laid
And thereby made the allied fleet aware
That westward prowled the British, unafraid

Of greater numbers, of their fate in war,
Of shoal, or storm or wreck or any ill
From battle off an enemy lee shore.
His watch continued through the night until

An eastward low grey line at break of day
Brailed up to raise the curtain on the play.

200   A hazy morning and a sleepy swell   *21 Oct 1805*
Which slowly broached upon the Spanish shore
Were stage and lighting for the peaceful spell,
A six hours overture, before the roar

Of cannon at mid-day began the fight.
And men were calm if fearful of their fate
As ships moved gently in the growing light
Before a breeze which tended to abate.

To port and starboard British warships spread
Their studding sails to pilfer every breath
Of north-west wind to carry them ahead
And hasten to their rendezvous with death.

Thus Nelson's twenty seven vessels bore
In line towards Villeneuve's jumbled thirty four.

TRAFALGAR

201 At six a.m. when Villeneuve descried   *21 Oct 1805*
The British strength he signalled to his fleet
To wear and sail north-east, a tactic tried,
Too late, to save the line of his retreat.

"Perdidos!" "Lost!" A Spanish captain snapped
His telescope's extension, thinking rout
Would follow for an allied fleet entrapped
In its own muddle as it turned about.

From sailing for the Straits in ragged line
The French and Spaniards swung, a demi-lune
Inclined towards home, inviting Nelson's chine,
Inducing Collingwood's attack at noon.

Two blows to split a straggling fleet in three
And let its van drift on impotently.

202 As Collingwood in "Royal Sovereign" shaved
He bade his servant glance across the sea
To glimpse a sight for evermore engraved
On his and every seaman's memory.

The greatest force of sailing warships known,
Three nations' navies, filled that sea with ships
Converging slowly, by a small wind blown
On canvas clouds which threatened to eclipse

The local skies. Strict Collingwood advised
An officer to change his boots for shoes
And silken stockings for he realised
That eased the surgeon's work; while Nelson's crews

Had further comforts; surgeons were informed
The Admiral wished all knives and saws be warmed.

TRAFALGAR

203   The hours of waiting offered Nelson chance   *21 Oct 1805*
To write a witnessed footnote to his will,
A plea for State provision to enhance
His care for Emma but that codicil

Did nothing for his mistress or his child.
They were "his country's legacy". So dear
To him that new anxiety beguiled
A barren hope that sprang from present fear,

Not for himself but pressingly for those
It was his natural duty to defend.
He knew his government's self-righteous pose
And judged that natural justice in the end

Would not be done, conventionally denied,
With spendthrift Emma stranded if he died.

204   His faith from childhood brought him to his knees
To pray in private when he also penned
Before the fleets engaged his measured pleas
For victory, justice and that none offend

In victory by ill-conduct. Britain's cause
Was Europe's "benefit", the key to bring
An end to Europe's fratricidal wars.
In this great prayer he humbly stove to sing

The praises of the "great God I adore".
He prayed for "glorious victory" yet he saw
Pursuit of glory only was a flaw
Which added to the awful cost of war.

In any reckoning of human life
Lost ethics added to the price of strife.

TRAFALGAR

205 The British closed for action, all decks cleared; *21 Oct 1805*
  The livestock, sties and coops flung overboard;
  Cooks fires put out as hostile vessels neared
  And furniture stowed deep in holds or stored

  In boats astern. On gun decks seamen stripped
  To waists to lessen sweat and stop a shirt
  Abrading wounds with threads if splinters ripped,
  So giving better chance to heal the hurt.

  Bandanas bound mens heads and brows to save
  Their eyes from sweat, their ears from thunderous sound.
  Cold meat and bread were issued and rum gave
  That fillip which the Dutch used to confound

  The fear all feel. In "Victory" instead
  Of rum half pints of wine combatted dread.

206 The stimulus of music was employed
  To rouse men's spirits and in "Bucentaure",
  The flagship of the French, the crew enjoyed
  The 'Ca Ira', cried 'Vive l'Empereur' and saw

  Their metal eagle carried on parade,
  A talisman set up beside a mast.
  In "Victory" 'Rule Britannia' was played
  And Nelson with his frigate captains passed

  Along each deck with Hardy to be seen
  And inspire trust while seeming to inspect
  A polished ship, most scrupulously clean,
  All cannon double shotted and correct

  With sponges, rammers, handspikes, wads and shot
  Precisely placed on an alloted spot.

TRAFALGAR

207 Two men danced hornpipes in the idle spell   *21 Oct 1805*
When every preparation had been made
To kill their foes. A third was heard to tell
His mate their prizes once the game was played

Would give them both "good money and a cruise
Amongst the girls", while Nelson said he wished
To send the fleet a signal "to amuse"
The waiting men. Lieutenant Pascoe fished

Among the coded hoists but said "confides"
And "Nelson" needed extra flags. Instead
He found a flag for "England" and besides
A two flagged word "expects". The signal read

Immortally that every man should do
His duty as he was expected to.

208 The British frigates working parallel
To Collingwood and Nelson when they turned
Repeated signals so that all could tell
What Nelson's signals were if not discerned

Beyond the next ahead, through cannon smoke
Through veiling sails or tumbled masts and yards.
His morning spent on "Victory" Blackwood spoke
To Nelson, thinking fourteen on the cards

When asked how many prizes would become
New British ships. That did not satisfy
The Admiral who cavilled at the sum.
His bargain was for twenty. Bade "Good bye."

When frigate captains left he smiled and then
"God bless you, Blackwood. We shan't meet again."

TRAFALGAR

209   With wind abeam the French and Spaniards made   *21 Oct 1805*
A sluggish knot an hour. The British urged
Their vessels faster as the weak breeze played
Upon their quarters while the fleets converged

For square rigged ships attain a greater speed
The more their course can bring the wind abaft,
Or handier crews can trim, or less the weed
And barnacles they tow. Clean bottomed craft

Outsail all others and when Collingwood
Swung "Royal Sovereign" out of line to lead
The lee division's thrust his captains could
Not match his new sheathed copper bottomed speed.

"See now that noble fellow!" Nelson said
As "Royal Sovereign" into action led.

210   The van, or weather line which "Victory" led
Maintained its course with Nelson fully dressed
In Admiral's uniform. He shook his head
When asked to change as orders on his breast

Blazed out his rank. His calm "It is too late
To shift a coat," a vanity designed
To steel his courage and embrace that fate
Embroiled in glory which possessed his mind.

His golden orb's refulgence glowed beyond
The listless tricolours, the gold and red
Of Spanish ensigns, yet sustained his fond
Relationship with all the men he led.

Part actor posturing upon his stage
Part fanning peacock posed within his cage.

TRAFALGAR

211 This clothed his leadership, such brag a way   *21 Oct 1805*
Of overcoming fear. His Norfolk drawl
Now put the weather squadron into play
As "Victory" swung to Hardy's burring bawl,

A hard West Country captain, strong and tall
To counterpoint his Admiral's nasal twang
And Eastern Counties wiriness. His call
To helmsmen through the whispering "Victory" rang.

The slushing of the sea and riggings' squeak
Of rope on block or halyards lazy slat,
A flag or sail's faint flap and timbers' creak
Were instruments which played to men whose chat

Was silenced by command as "Victory" bore
Most dangerously bows on for "Bucentaure".

212 The dreaded likelihood of being raked
From stem to stern by concentrated fire
Of broadsides was the gamble Nelson staked
To break the line, contriving to inspire

All British captains following astern.
He knew French fire was usually aimed
At masts and sails, a ploy designed to earn
Free movement when an enemy was maimed.

Yet poor ship handling and a lack of skill
In gunnery reduced the British risk
Who, firing on the down roll, aimed to kill
By riddling hulls. French long range fire was brisk,

Killed twenty and broke "Victory's" mizzen top
With fifty hits. Her charge it failed to stop.

TRAFALGAR

213   Upon a strengthening swell the "Victory" steered   21 Oct 1805
      Still mute in face of French and Spanish fire
      Her aim to pass astern of what appeared
      To be the centre's lead ship and acquire

      Two strangleholds, a noose of British power
      Around the centre and the allied rear
      And so discount the leeward van whose hour
      Of opportunity was lost through fear

      Or indecision or a signal fault
      Not reading Villeneuve's order to return
      As silent "Victory" slowing to a halt
      Unleashed a broadside through the flagship's stern

      A fiery vomit which wrecked "Bucentaure"
      And killed at once a hundred men or more.

214   Confronted by a hedge of masts ahead
      The "Victory's" option was to run aboard
      A Spanish ship or "Redoubtable" instead
      And Hardy asked "Which shall I choose, my Lord?"

      "Choose for yourself", was Nelson's quiet reply
      As British warships piled into a scrum
      Of jostling ships. He knew that, live or die,
      Their rapid fire would win the fight to come.

      A "pell-mell battle" had been his desire.
      He had it now as three decked "Victory" smashed
      Against the two decked French ship and the fire
      Of broadside after broadside flashed and crashed

      Around the tiny Lucas on his poop
      A Gallic fighting cock upon his coop.

TRAFALGAR

215　　A fearsome dwarf, cock hatted, newly shaved　　*21 Oct 1805*
　　　With polished boots, immaculately dressed,
　　　Lucas, a-strut, raved at his crew and waved
　　　A shortened sword. His attitudes expressed

　　　The fiery soul of France. His men were trained
　　　In boarding tactics and his yards were manned
　　　By seamen with grenades who had attained
　　　An extra skill as marksmen. Nelson banned

　　　The use of small arms from the masts for fear
　　　Of needless casualties from long range fire;
　　　Now tangled yards of "Redoubtable" were near
　　　The "Victory's" upper deck, her marksmen higher.

　　　Thus Hardy, calm amid the cannon's blast,
　　　Heard Nelson say "They've done for me at last."

216　　Instinctively he knew he had no hope
　　　Shot down through epaulette and breast and back
　　　Yet ordered that a shredded tiller rope
　　　He saw shot frayed should be renewed. His rack

　　　Of pain began when lifted. Some have said
　　　His kerchief cloaked his orders to conceal
　　　His downfall from his crew but as he bled
　　　Strong Seckers, Sergeant of Marines, could feel

　　　His Admiral's limpness on the slippery wood
　　　Of a companionway well soaked in blood
　　　Down steps on which two swaying seaman stood
　　　To help them to the cockpit. Little good

　　　Could surgery do. "Tend those whom you can save."
　　　He ordered. Conduct of the very brave.

TRAFALGAR

217   Soon Nelson's diagnosis was confirmed   *21 Oct 1805*
By Surgeon Beatty as he lay beside
The cockpit wall which Chaplain Scott affirmed
A shambles. Limbs were severed and men died

As ceaselessly Scott rubbed his master's hand
Or gave him lemonade to sip or fanned
The foetid air or tried to understand
The murmurs of a man who said he'd planned

For twenty ships' surrender. Hardy spoke
Above the constant thunder of the guns
To say fourteen had struck. The jarring oak
Spoke also with increasing lifts and runs

That told a dying seaman of the need
To "Anchor, Hardy. Anchor," with all speed.

218   He left, he said, the legacy behind
Of Lady Hamilton for whom the State
Should care. As numbness grew and strength declined
He felt his "sins had not been very great."

His golden orb was not a candle blown
Its gleam and brightness does not wax or wane
Its steady beam to all men since has shown
The course to steer through danger, fear and pain.

"Thank God I've done my duty," was his theme
Repeatedly pronounced. As darkness grew
Hard Hardy came and knelt. As in a dream
When asked brushed lips on forehead. Nelson knew

That tough commander loved him. As he died
The storm arose, guns hushed and brave men cried.

BIBLIOGRAPHY

ENGLISH

The Life of Nelson: Robert Southey *John Murray 1830*
Nelson: Carola Oman *Hodder & Stoughton 1947*
Nelson's Band of Brothers: Ludovic Kennedy *Odhams 1952*
Nelson: Oliver Warner *Weidenfeld & Nicholson 1975*
The Nelson Touch (Anthology of Letters): Clemence Dane *Heinemann 1942*
Nelson's First Love: Patrick Delaforce *Bishopsgate Press 1988*
The Years of Endurance: Arthur Bryant *Collins 1942*
Years of Victory: Arthur Bryant *Collins 1944*
The Price of Admiralty: John Keegan *Hutchinson 1988*
Statesmen and Sea Power: Admiral Sir Herbert Richmond *Clarendon Press 1946*
England Under the Hanoverians: Sir Charles Grant Robertson *Methuen 1911*
A History of Modern Europe: C. A. Fyffe *Cassell 1895*
Men o' War (John Jervis): Captain Taprell Dorling RN *Philip Allan 1929*
Sir John Moore: Carola Oman *Hodder & Stoughton 1953*
The History of Napoleon Buonaparte: J G Lockhart *1829. J M Dent 1906*
Bombing & Strategy – The Fallacy of Total War (Admiral Calder): Admiral Sir Gerald Dickens *Sampson, Low, Marston 1947*
The Anatomy of Courage: Lord Moran
Clausewitz: Michael Howard *Oxford University Press 1980*
Nelson's Navy 1793–1815: Brian Lavery *Conway Maritime Press 1990*
The Decisive Battles of the Western World 1792–1944: Maj. Gen. J F C Fuller *Eyre & Spottiswood 1954*
Encyclopaedia Britannica: *Encyc. Brit. Inc. Chicago 1947*

FRENCH

Marines et Revolution: Martine Acerra & Jean Meyer *Editions Ouest-France 1988*
Les Marins de Napoleon: Auguste Thomazi *Librarie Jules Tallandier Paris 1978*
Brest. Un Port en Revolution 1789–1799: Philippe Henwood & Edmond Monage *Editions Ouest-France 1989*
Saint-Malo. Cite Corsaire: Therese Herpin *Editions Alsatia Paris 1950*
Ahmed le Boucher: Edouard Lockroy *Ollendorf, Paris c 1875*
Servitude et Grandeurs Militaires: Alfred de Vigny *La Revue de Deux Mondes 1835 & Classiques Garnier 1955*

Facts and ideas have been drawn from visits to:

The National Maritime Museum, Greenwich
H.M.S. Victory
The Royal Naval Museum, Portsmouth
The Royal Marines Museum, Eastleigh
The Nelson Museum, Monmouth
La Musee de la Marine, Brest
La Musee de la Marine, Rochefort
La Musee de la Marine, Toulon

The helpfulness of the National Maritime Museum far surpassed my highest hopes and The Chairman of Trustees, Admiral of the Fleet Lord Lewin, Professor Pieter Van der Merwe, David Spence and Christopher Gray could not have been kinder.

The enthusiastic encouragement and advice of Dr A L Rowse; the corrections and suggestions of Robert Roberts and help by Commander John Morton Lee OBE RN (Retd) and Lt Commander A L Bleby RN (Retd) are acknowledged with gratitude.

Production owes much to Ranjit Rai-Quantrill, covers designs; Amanda Mitchell, my daughter, art work; and Michael Coates, typography.

THE NELSON TOUCH

On 13 Sep 1805, Nelson left his family and home for the last time yet amid stress and bustle he tried to secure benefit for a naval widow, writing to the First Lord of the Admiralty, Lord Barham

"My Lord,

The friends and widow of Dr. John Snipe, late physician to the Mediterranean Fleet are desirous that I should testify to your Lordship his character which I have great pleasure in doing for a better man in private life nor a more able man in his profession I never met with and I much fear his death was principally owing to his going to Messina for the purpose of buying lemon juice for the fleet at Home which is likely to be obtained at 1/-6 pence per gallon instead of 8 shillings.

I am with great respect your Lordship's most obedient servant,

Nelson & Bronte"